Madness, Magic, and Medicine

The Treatment and Mistreatment of the Mentally Ill

Madness, Magic, and Medicine

The Treatment and Mistreatment of the Mentally Ill

Elinor Lander Horwitz

J. B. Lippincott Company
Philadelphia and New York

362.2

77-03987

D [handwritten] 10/17/77 6.95

With special thanks to Norman, Bob, and Earle

U.S. Library of Congress Cataloging in Publication Data

Horwitz, Elinor Lander.
  Madness, magic, and medicine: the treatment and mistreatment of the mentally ill.

  Bibliography: p.
  Includes index.
  SUMMARY: Discusses the treatment of the mentally ill through the ages.
  1. Mentally ill—Care and treatment—History—Juvenile literature. [1. Mentally ill—Care and treatment—History] I. Title. [DNLM: 1. Mental disorders—Therapy. 2. Mental disorders—History. W M400 H824m] RC388.H67   362.2'09   76-54760
ISBN-0-397-31723-9

For my parents

Contents

1   *Encaged and Chained*   9

2   *Medicine Men, Prophets, and the Healing Touch*   14

3   *Hippocrates and the Humors: Ancient Greece and Rome*   25

4   *The Middle Ages: Faith, Superstition, Exorcism*   39

5   *Witchcraft and Sorcery*   56

6   *Trials and Treatments in Colonial America*   65

7   *The Lunatic Asylum*   78

8   *Phrenology and Mesmerism*   100

9   *Psychoanalysis: The Modern Era*   115

10   *Electroshock, Psychopharmacology, Psychosurgery*   131

11   *Other Contemporary Therapies*   154

12   *The Full Benefits of Our Society*   171

    Suggestions for Further Reading   185

    Index   188

William Norris in his cell at Bedlam. From a drawing by George Cruikshank. National Library of Medicine, Bethesda, Md.

1
Encaged and Chained

In one of the cells, the Committee saw William Norris. He stated himself to be 55 years of age and that he had been confined about fourteen years in consequence of attempting to defend himself from what he conceived to be the improper treatment of his keeper. He was confined in the manner the Committee saw him, namely—a stout iron ring was riveted round his neck, from which a short chain passed to a ring, made to slide upward or downward on an upright massive iron bar inserted into the wall; round his body a strong iron bar, about two inches wide, was riveted; on each side of the bar was a circular projection enclosing each of his arms, pinioning them close to his sides; this waist bar was secured by two similar bars, which passing over his shoulders, were riveted to the waist bar, both before and behind; the iron ring round his neck was connected to the bars on his shoulders by a double link; from each of these bars another short chain passed to the ring on the upright bar. We were told he was enabled to raise himself so as to stand against the wall, but it was impossible for him to advance from the wall in which the iron bar is soldered, on account of the shortness of the chain— and equally impossible for him to repose in any other position than on his back. His right leg was chained to the trough, in which he had remained thus encaged and chained more than twelve years.

> from the report of the Voluntary Sub-Committee on Investigation of Lunatic Asylums by William Hone. Submitted to the House of Commons in 1815.

Nothing is known of William Norris's life previous to his confinement in London's Bethlehem Hospital—widely known as "Bedlam." William Hone, who left this record, was a pamphleteer and reformer who, with his friend, the famous illustrator George Cruikshank, made a personal survey of conditions in the lunatic asylums of England in the years 1814 and 1815. His report led to a parliamentary investigation and some specific legislation regarding methods of restraint of mental patients in British asylums.

At the time of the investigation William Norris's case was commonplace, not exceptional. Although there have been brief periods in history when a minority of the mentally ill were afforded concerned treatment, most often they have been brutally abused or neglected. Throughout the ages theories about the *causes* of mental illness have shaped social and legal attitudes toward the insane and dictated the therapy—or lack of therapy— provided by families and communities. In periods when mental illness was thought to be incurable, the insane were chained at home, in prisons, or in asylums, or simply run out of town. When it was considered possible to cure the afflicted of their illness, therapies were devised which may seem sadistic, grotesque, ignorant, or hostile but which reflect some optimism on the part of physicians, priests, or medicine men.

Historically, exorcism of one variety or another has been the most prevalent of all treatments for mental illness, because belief in possession by demons or spirits as the cause of irrational behavior has been far the most common theory in all countries of the world. Neither the belief nor the practice has ever completely died out, and people still seek cures through the help of religious or lay faith healers. When the causes of madness were thought to be organic, rather than mystical or magical, patients were treated in accordance with medical theories and practices of the time. In periods when psychological theories were put forth as explanations of the causes of mental illness, patients have been treated with various forms of psychotherapy.

In the twentieth century an unprecedented rate of scientific advance in psychiatric and biochemical understanding of mental illness has led to a wide range of new and varied therapies which—in the light of today's social philosophy—are being offered to an ever-increasing number of people in broad community programs. "Mental illness" is now seen as a spectrum of diseases with many different causes, treatable by a constantly expanding repertoire of therapeutic approaches. Most have cruder precedents in earlier pre-scientific treatments. Occupational and recreation therapy have been widely recommended since ancient times for their effectiveness in releasing tensions and suppressed emotions. The benefits of listening to music, of dancing, of agricultural labor have been "discovered" and "rediscovered" in very different cultures. Psychosurgery and electroshock therapy have primitive precedents in the use of the trephine to open the head and the relaying of shocks from electric eels. The therapeutic use of drugs is as old as the history of man. In periods when mental illness was viewed as resulting at least partially from environmental pressures—a notion not new to this century—sufferers were removed to asylums and encouraged to discuss their fears and sorrows with a therapist individually or in groups.

Unlike other mistreated minorities, the insane are totally vulnerable and totally helpless. Few can act or speak out in their own defense. An unlimited potential for abuse of power has resided in the person authorized to judge another insane and to determine his treatment. Historically, this has not usually been a physician but rather some civil or religious authority. Today we speak of the *right* to receive therapy or to reject therapy—considerations which have broad medical, legal, and moral implications. Concerns of this sort are unquestionably new to our time.

William Norris's cruel confinement in "Bedlam" happened long ago, and we are now living in an infinitely more humane, enlightened, and scientific era. We do not chain lunatics to the walls of cells. In fact, we do not like to hear the term "lunatic" used because to our contemporary sensibilities it sounds cruel and denigrating. Actually, we don't even approve of the terms "insane" and "insanity." We prefer to speak of "mental illness"—a designation which has no moral overtones at all, no suggestion that the afflicted are in any way less deserving of sympathy and the highest level of medical attention than people who are physically ill.

And yet scarcely a year passes without revelations in our newspapers of scandalously inhumane treatment of the mentally ill or the mentally retarded in our private and public institutions. Outraged citizens and their elected representatives in government demand that something be done, and often specific improvements take place. Yet when financial priorities are at issue, the mentally ill continue to be the losers. A disturbed member of the family is often viewed as a source of acute embarrassment, a person whose career may be permanently destroyed even if recovery seems complete. Despite intensive efforts at public education—and despite the fact that health officials tell us that one in ten Americans can be expected to be hospitalized for mental illness during his or her lifetime—the subject remains one to which most people bring their most primitive fears and unreasoning prejudices. A survey of the history of the treatment of the mentally ill reveals that this has always been the case.

2
Medicine Men, Prophets, and the Healing Touch

Some physical diseases are international; others occur only in restricted areas. Certain nutritional, parasitic, and viral conditions are found in epidemic proportions in one area of the world and are unknown elsewhere. Plagues which devastated past civilizations have mysteriously disappeared and never returned. Other illnesses which are common today may be of relatively recent origin. Syphilis, which was first reported in Spain at the end of the fifteenth century, rapidly spread through Europe and is now prevalent in most parts of the world. Leprosy was so rampant in western Europe in the late Middle Ages that Paris alone had several hundred leprosariums; since the fifteenth century it has appeared almost exclusively in tropical and subtropical regions and is considered one of the least contagious illnesses.

Mental illness, however, has been known to all peoples throughout history. World Health Organization studies suggest that the statistical incidence of the major mental illnesses—the psychoses—is virtually the same in all countries. Although anthropologists warn of the difficulties and dangers of trying to define "normal" or "abnormal" behavior in cultures very different from our own, the fact remains that all societies recognize certain acts or utterances among their own people as symptoms of mental derangement. It is only the symptoms that differ. If an American college president suddenly became intensely fearful of assault by evil spirits we might deem him insane. And yet, the same diagnosis could be made of a member of a primitive tribe if he were to deny the spirit world. Tales of madmen are found in the legends, literature, and historical accounts of cultures which flourished thousands of years before the Christian Era. From carvings on stone steles we learn of cases of mental aberration and of miraculous cures effected by the gods of Egypt in 2500 B.C. Studies of primitive tribes still in existence in remote areas of the world shed light on attitudes toward the insane and rituals for alleviating mental disorders in ancient pre-literate societies.

The history of the treatment of mental illness begins with the magico-religious rites of primitive people and extends to the broad spectrum of current psychological and physiological approaches. Today most of us believe that the diagnosis and treatment of insanity are the proper province of the medical specialist, but this view has prevailed only in recent centuries. Through most of history the healer has been part priest and part magician—a man or woman thought to be able to bridge the gap between the physical world and the world of evil spirits, which were believed to cause all illness, physical and mental. The oldest representation of a healer, a painting from 15,000 B.C. on the wall of a cave in southern France, shows a priestly figure wearing deer antlers.

Although people of all eras have feared illness, primitive man lived in a state of physical and emotional insecurity that is difficult for us to imagine. His life was constantly challenged by forces and dangers over which he had no control. Wild beasts attacked him as he hunted for food. Extremes of weather killed his crops, his cattle, and his family. Accidents and illnesses for which there was no relief and no remedy posed a constant menace. He lived in a world threatened by evil spirits who might, at any time, invade and take command of his body or his wits and propel him to his doom.

The belief in malignant spirits may seem ignorant and fanciful today, but to primitive man it was an attempt to give rational explanation to what was otherwise an impenetrable puzzle. If a man was hit by a stone and felt pain, no mystery of cause and effect was involved. But if his perfectly sensible son suddenly—for no apparent reason —began behaving in a peculiar manner and making strange statements, the only "logical" explanation of the change was invasion of his being by invisible forces. The medicine man or prophet or shaman charged with expelling such forces was a religious official selected because of his skill in contacting the world of the spirits, who could then speak or act through him. He was both healer and divinator— a man who diagnosed and cured illnesses, predicted the future, and also handled such odd jobs as making rain and locating goats or sheep who had strayed from the flock. Faith in the magical powers of the tribal healer was unquestioning. He was the highest authority to whom one might appeal in times of crisis.

The tribal healer attained his prestigious position because of special characteristics which marked him as different from ordinary men. He might have a physical abnormality —extra fingers or toes or teeth. Epilepsy was often viewed as a sign of divine designation among ancient people and was referred to by the Greeks of the classical era as the "sacred disease." The most important mark of the healer was his ability to attain a state of inspired frenzy in which he went into an ecstatic trance, lost control of his voluntary movements, and—at the height of his excitement—experienced visual and auditory hallucinations.

When the shaman contacted the spirits he might extract a stone or other object from his own mouth or that of the victim to symbolize the escape of evil spirits—and the patient, who confidently expected such a result, often experienced total relief of symptoms. Sacrifices of various sorts might then be made to seal the cure. In some instances the cure involved rites in which the spirits—and therefore the symptoms—were transferred to another being, usually an animal. It is from this practice that we derive the word "scapegoat," meaning one who takes on the guilt or burdens of others.

Although he was charged with the duty of healing, the primitive shaman, like the Hebrew prophets of the Old Testament, the early Christian mystics, and the dervishes of the East, exhibited types of personal behavior we readily associate with insanity. Ethnologists who study primitive tribes debate this point and many believe that shamans are indeed deranged personalities who act out their instabilities in their ceremonial duties. And yet the distinction between the frenzied healer who hears voices and sees visions and the mentally disturbed tribesman he attempts to cure seems to be that the shaman is possessed by helpful rather than evil spirits. He is also expected to behave in a controlled and rational fashion when not performing his duties. Many religions, particularly those of Eastern origin, hold that it is necessary to attain a state of exhilaration or trance in order to contact the transcendent world and gain audience with the deity. The ability to do so is highly esteemed.

Non-inspirational healers—the ancestors of the physician —had their own methods of dealing with swellings, fever, or dementia. In ancient Peru and in the countries of the eastern Mediterranean in North Africa, trephination was a commonly employed last-ditch treatment designed to liberate the body from tormenting demons if the shaman's ministrations failed. Small holes, rarely more than two centimeters in diameter, were bored in the skull of the sufferer. Skulls four to five thousand years old with holes made by the trephine—a primitive drill—have been found in many parts of the world. Scientists believe that the operation was intended to provide an easy exit route for evil spirits, that it was rarely fatal, and that in problems such as brain tumor or head injury when symptoms were due to pressure of an expanded or swollen brain against the skull, relief of symptoms must actually have occurred.

The ancient Egyptians, Persians, and Babylonians, as well as the people of India and China, wrote of mental illness and the intrusive demons who caused the distress. The Persians listed 99,999 diseases in their Venidad and attributed all to evil spirits. The so-called Ebers Papyrus and the Edward Smith Papyrus, both dating from about 1550 B.C., offer evidence of the Egyptians' view of supernatural causes of disease and point to the brain as the site of mental functions. The ancient Egyptians also sought help for the sick from those skilled in dream interpretation. Unlike twentieth-century psychoanalysts, who interpret dreams as relating to the patient's past, earlier authorities invariably considered dreams to be portents of the future. The Egyptians sent sufferers who had not improved on pilgrimages to shrines and temples, as the

Greeks and Christians would do in later centuries. Imhotep was an actual physician who lived about 3000 B.C. Many centuries after his death he was worshipped as the Egyptian god of medicine. Many cures of physical and mental illness were reported at his temple in Memphis.

Early Hindus wrote of seven kinds of demoniac possession: five angers of devils, one of the gods, one of the spirits of the dead. When the gods were angered they entered a person and produced mental disease. The holy books, the Vedas, and a later book, the Characa, tell of healing by sorcerers and prescribe chanting, fasting, songs, purification ceremonies, herbs, and kind treatment as additional therapies. The ancient Chinese saw deviation from filial duties as a cause of insanity and priestly exorcists held ceremonies to appease dead ancestors while physicians tried acupuncture. A folk belief still found in rural areas of China and Japan holds that the fox can cause mental disturbances.

The prophets of the Old Testament were, like the shamans of primitive tribes, skilled in hearing voices and seeing visions. They too were regarded with veneration because of such signs of religious vocation. It is difficult to evaluate the mental stability of these holy men who, in full prophetic frenzy, shrieked mysterious words, tore at their garments, fell rolling to the ground, lost consciousness, shook, twirled about like whirlwinds, and seemed to spend a good bit of their time in the most violent state of physical and mental agitation. They dressed in sackcloth, or like Isaiah, went barefoot and naked about the streets for periods of years. Their obedience to the word of the deity as they interpreted it was more than strict, it was fanatical, as they burst in on peaceful scenes to bring unwelcome prophecies of doom. And yet they also performed everyday duties as they healed the sick, listened sympathetically to tales of bereavement, returned lost property.

To the monotheistic Hebrew of the Old Testament, mental aberration of both holy and unholy forms resulted from having been touched by the Lord. God could turn a man into an inspired prophet, who thereafter was able to relay his word—or he could inflict madness as punishment for disobedience, for sexual misdeed, uncleanliness, or idleness. In Deuteronomy, Moses lists the curses that will settle on those who disobey God's commandments and among them is the warning that, "The Lord shall smite thee with madness and blindness, and astonishment of heart."

Because it was thought that madness came from God, the insane were allowed to wander about free of harm. The Old Testament storytellers wrote of the feigned madness of David, who fled the homicidal fury of King Saul and found himself in the kingdom of Achish, the king of Gath. Gath was the city of the giant Goliath, whom David had vanquished some years earlier. Realizing that he had run from one dangerous situation to another, David pretended to be demented. He made strange markings on the doors of the gate, and, the storytellers relate, he "let his spittle fall down upon his beard." King Achish, who seems to have been familiar with these symptoms—and who, in later histories, is said to have had an insane wife and daughter—looked upon this behavior with dismay. He reminded his servants that there were already enough unbalanced people in the kingdom: "Lo, ye see the man is mad: wherefore than have ye brought him to me? Have I need of madmen..." David was released to go his way in safety.

One of the most moving tales in the Old Testament is

the story of King Saul, a man summoned by God and then—because of his disobedience—abandoned and punished. The story of Saul's madness is also the earliest written account of music therapy. Music made by harps, tambourines, cymbals, and voices always accompanied festivities in Old Testament times. In addition to being aesthetically pleasing, it was valued as a means of enhancing emotion, exciting religious ecstasy, and quieting the disturbed mind.

In the Old Testament tale, God commanded Saul to destroy the people known as the Amalekites—to slay their king and all their men and animals. But the defiant ruler took King Agag of Amalek alive and spared the best of the flocks as spoil for his men, and God, the source of all fortune, good and evil, struck Saul down. From that day onward—until he slew himself with his own sword—King Saul was troubled with fits of deep depression, paranoia, and uncontrollable rage. Although his madness was viewed as incurable he was offered some relief. The young David, slayer of Goliath, was brought to the king to play his harp. "And it came to pass, when the evil spirit from God was upon Saul, that David took a harp, and played with his hand; so Saul was refreshed and was well, and the evil spirit departed from him." The treatment proved only temporarily effective, and when the mad king's frenzy led him to attempt to slay the harpist, David fled.

Another dramatic reference to insanity in the Old Testament deals with the bizarre form of mental illness which came upon Nebuchadnezzar, the king who founded the second Babylonian Empire at the site of the ruins of ancient Assyria in the sixth century B.C. In the Book of Daniel we are told of the illness that visited Nebuchadnezzar in his later years, when the king imagined himself to be a beast. He left his wondrous palace to wander in the fields with the cattle, where he fed on grass and led the unsheltered life of an animal. "And his body was wet with the dew of heaven, till his hairs were grown like eagles' feathers, and his nails like birds' claws." In the Old Testament version of his life, the king suffered this madness for seven years as punishment for pride.

Nebuchadnezzar was afflicted with a form of insanity familiar to the ancients. The physicians of the Middle Ages and the Renaissance called it lycanthropy. Although the term refers to transformation of a human being into a wolf—or "werewolf"—it is also used to describe any case of insanity in which the victim believes himself to have turned into an animal and begins to behave accordingly. Apparently this psychotic delusion was relatively common in countries and in times when such transformations were believed to actually happen. When belief in werewolves became uncommon, the delusion disappeared from case histories of the insane.

The notion that human beings can assume the appearance and behavior of a particular animal is very ancient and persisted in remote parts of the world until recent centuries. Legends of men who assume animal form usually focus on the most feared beast of the region. In India and southeast Asia men and women were said to have turned into tigers; in Africa a lion or leopard or hyena has been more common; in South America legends center on the jaguar, and in parts of Scandinavia, the bear. Although the animal chosen is usually menacing and carnivorous, transformations into cattle, birds, cats, dogs, pigs, and deer also appear in both written and oral folklore.

Tales of transformation into beasts have a peculiar

horrifying fascination. The transformation, according to legend, can be temporary or permanent, voluntary or involuntary. The victim suddenly begins to walk on all fours and to crave foods consumed by beasts, including the flesh of dead or even living bodies. Voluntary transformations were said to be accomplished by putting on an animal skin, rubbing the body with magical ointments, and then eating an animal's brains or drinking water from its footprints. The return to human form was effected by removing the skin, having your baptismal name shouted three times, and being greeted by a person who makes the sign of the cross. Belief in such transformations persisted in France until the nineteenth century, when there were still occasional tales of sightings of the *loup-garou* in remote regions. In eighteenth-century Russia, during the final year of a long war with Sweden, country people believed that the wolves in northern regions were Swedish prisoners who had escaped and become transformed.

Saul and Nebuchadnezzar are the two most famous victims of madness in the Old Testament. Later Hebrew writings in a book of laws called the Talmud speak with greater sophistication of mental illness, differentiating it from mental deficiency and from physically based mental problems such as the delirium of fever. It is interesting to note that in the Talmud the Rabbis include as beneficial approaches recreational activity and encouraging the victime to talk about his troubles.

In the New Testament insanity, which is still viewed as punishment for sin, is instantly cured by Jesus. The method of treatment is laying on of the hands. Both Luke and Mark tell of the madman of Gadarene who had "an unclean spirit" and who "had devils long time and ware no clothes, neither abode in any house, but in the tombs."

Jesus and his apostles came upon this savage madman who could not be bound because, in his frenzy and fury, he was possessed of unnatural strength and was able to break all fetters. "And always, night and day, he was in the mountains and in the tombs, crying and cutting himself with stones," the Gospel tells us. When asked his name the man answered, "My name is Legion: for we are many." Jesus, touched by mercy, promptly effected a magical cure—transferring the devils who had plagued the man into a herd of swine feeding on a nearby mountain. The bedeviled animals rushed down a precipice into the sea and drowned. The former madman is last seen fully clothed and sitting at the feet of the Savior—to the astonishment and awe of the local populace. The story inspired uncounted numbers of cures by faith in later centuries.

3

Hippocrates and the Humors: Ancient Greece and Rome

It was in ancient Greece and Rome that treatment of the insane first became the concern of physicians. Madness was stripped of myth and magic—and poetry—and turned into a bodily illness, most appropriately treated by accepted medical techniques and remedies. The enlightened outlook of Greek and Roman physicians influenced the treatment of a small number of wealthy and sophisticated citizens of the time and later became the most reactionary force in the history of psychiatry. Over two thousand years after the death of Hippocrates, medical schools—in total disregard of anatomical and physiological discoveries of the sixteenth and seventeenth centuries—continued to preach his theories and remedies. Greek dicta about noxious body humors and their effect on mental health were cited as enduring truths by doctors in colonial America and were considered suitable justification for such remedies as purging and bleeding as late as the nineteenth century.

A discussion of classical Greek and Roman medicine must begin with the myths, legends, and literature of earlier times, which dealt repeatedly with tales of insanity and shaped a body of folk belief on the subject. The daughters of Proetus, king of Argos, were punished for refusing to worship Dionysus. The maidens believed themselves to be cows and descended on all fours into the pasture, lowing as they grazed. They were cured by a seer named Malampus, who understood the language of the birds from whom he learned all manner of secrets and mysteries. In the Homeric legends, written about 1000 B.C., attacks of insanity almost invariably foreshadow a tragic end. Ajax, the Greek hero of the Trojan War, appears in the *Iliad* and the *Odyssey* as a formidable warrior. He fights the Trojan leader Hector in single combat and rescues the body of Achilles after the great leader is slain in battle. When Achilles's armor is given by Agammemnon to Odysseus, Ajax goes mad from disappointment and frustration and, in a fury, kills himself.

In other Greek tales madness comes as retribution for sin. As in the Old Testament, man's mind is thrown into disorder as punishment from above. Orestes, the son of Agammemnon and Clytemnestra, avenges the death of his father by slaying his mother and after this matricide he is pursued and driven mad by the Erinyes, who avenge violations of family honor and piety. Cleomenes of Sparta cuts down trees in the sacred grove of Ceres and Proserpine and bribes a Delphic priestess to utter a prophecy that will alarm his enemy. For this scandalous sacrilege he is punished with insanity and begins attacking people who pass him on the street. He is restrained by having his feet put in stocks, but when he convinces an attendant to give him a knife he stabs himself in a violent seizure of despair.

The Greeks, like the Hebrews, did not hold madmen responsible for their actions, and in their stories men feign madness when in danger, as David did in the land of Gath. Ulysses pretends to be mad to avoid having to go to the siege of Troy, yoking a bull and a horse together, an act any man would recognize as being thoroughly irrational. To make certain he gets the point across he then takes his strange team to the seashore and has them plow the sands.

In classical Greek civilization theatergoers saw madness portrayed in the plays of the great dramatists. These dramas reflected and reinforced popular attitudes about the supernatural causes of mental illness. Since most Greeks, schooled in the cherished legends, unquestioningly believed that madness sent by angry gods could not be cured by men, upper-class citizens who became ill were kept at home, guarded by servants. A small minority consulted physicians and were treated. The less fortunate deranged men and women of the lower economic classes were ignored or abused. Many people believed that the mentally ill could exert a malevolent influence on healthy men and women. It was common practice for passersby to spit on the ground as a charm against contagion if a madman passed. The custom persisted among the Romans and can be noted today among superstitious people in various parts of the world. The insane were kept in chains if they seemed menacing and if considered harmless were allowed to wander about the towns and on country lanes, often followed by taunting children or rough young men. Others sought help at the shrines of certain deities who were thought to have the power to cure madness. Sacrifices were made to Zeus during windy months when it was thought that bouts of insanity were likely to break out or recur. Astrologists noted that at times of the year when the heavenly bodies lay in certain relationships to one another the threat of madness was increased. The English word "lunacy"—used in medical and legal parlance until the twentieth century—reflects the ancient belief in the power of the moon (*luna* in Latin) over mental health.

To the Greek physicians mental illness was explainable only on a naturalistic organic basis and only physical treatments were considered valid. Disease, they said, comes from a disturbance of the proper workings of the body, and all mental and physical ills are of this same origin. Unlike the philosophers they did not view any form of madness as a blessing and they decried the magical beliefs and superstitions of the average man.

Their medical theory was based on a philosophy of nature. The world was thought to be composed of four elements—water, air, earth, and fire. The body, as a reflection of the world, was believed to be composed of four humors—blood, yellow bile, black bile, and phlegm—and personality was dependent on the relationship and dominance of the bodily humors. The four basic temperaments were the sanguine, the choleric, the melancholic, and the phlegmatic. The humors were thought to be manufactured in various organs of the body and each humor was said to have certain natural qualities of temperature and humidity. Disease occurred when imbalance or faulty interaction among the humors resulted from an excess of one humor and a corresponding unnatural degree of heat or cold or dryness or moistness. Chronic mental illness was considered—as it is today—less likely to be curable than the acute forms, but all varieties were explained by humoral activity.

The Greeks studied the symptoms of what we now call psychosis and divided insanity into two categories: melancholia and mania. Melancholia was a broad term which included all forms of unagitated depression and withdrawal. Mania referred to all of the more aggressive or violent types of psychoses. They believed that melancholy came from an excess of black bile and mania from an over-production of yellow bile. Prescribed treatment for either condition was purging and bleeding to drain off the overabundant humor, and also rest, a limited diet, gentle massage. If the patient seemed to be improving the diet was increased, exercise was prescribed, and sunbathing and alternating hot and cold baths were tried along with continued use of purgatives, cathartics, and bleeding.

The favorite purgative for the black bile of melancholics was black hellebore—a wild plant, which in overdoses is poisonous. This was such a common remedy that when a character in an Aristophanes play jeered at another, "Go to Anticyra," members of the audience knew he was really saying "You're a madman," since Anticyra was famed for its abundant crop of hellebore.

The rules for administering hellebore were complex. Since the effect was immediate and violent vomiting, physicians argued as to whether it should be taken before or after eating. Many felt it was important to know the mountain from which the dose had been gathered. Hellebore was often combined with other herbs and weeds to make an even stronger potion, and the learned physicians debated about treatments which might be used along with it. Some favored the use of strong scents to promote sneezing.

In addition to medicines and rest Greek doctors emphasized games, other recreational activities, and a slow progression of increasingly demanding mental exercises. Music was used to soothe patients and promote sleep, and opium was the favored sedative drug. A few physicians prescribed violent methods of cure—severe restraints, rigorous fasts, confinement in a dark room, dunkings in icy water, whipping, and excessive bleeding.

Magical cures had a much wider appeal than the gradual

routine of therapy suggested by physicians. They were available to all, rich and poor, and they were considered more rapidly curative. A night of frenzied participation in the Corybantic rites involving sacrifices to Dionysus and Cybele—who caused the problem to begin with—had been shown to be effective in many cases. A visit to a beautifully situated shrine was another alternative which many viewed more hopefully than treatment with medicines and rest. In ancient Greece many temples were built to the healing god Asklepios, whose symbol was the caduceus—a staff entwined by a snake. The device is still used to symbolize the medical profession. Like the Egyptian Imhotep, Asklepios was an actual physician who, long after his death, was worshipped as the god of medicine. The Asklepeion was a place of pilgrimage—a holy shrine and health spa combined, always situated with an inspirational view of mountains and valleys. After ritual purification the suffering supplicant, who might have any physical or mental disorder, went to sleep in an underground room of the temple. While he slept he was visited by the god Asklepios in his dream. The god would touch the afflicted person and the illness would be healed. In the morning an interpreter would discuss the dream with the patient, offering reminders if the patient was having difficulty recalling the details. He would make further curative suggestions—some people believe hypnotism was employed—and then offerings would be made to seal the cure.

All the ancient books on Greek medicine, which are our source of information on the subject, were formerly attributed to Hippocrates, the greatest physician of ancient Greece. Today these extensive writings are considered to be records of his own work and that of his contemporaries and followers as well. They form an archive of case histories, theories, and therapies.

Head of Asklepios. About 300 B.C. British Museum.

Hippocrates lived in the late fifth and early fourth centuries B.C. during the Golden Age of Greece, as a contemporary of Sophocles, Euripides, Pericles, Socrates, Phidias, Thucydides. It was the age when great masterpieces of drama, sculpture, and architecture were being created and when philosophical speculation pervaded all fields of endeavor. Hippocrates, who was trained in healing at a school in Cos near a medicinal spring, passed on to his followers the truly iconoclastic conviction that the gods had no power to cause physical and mental illnesses. In his landmark book on epilepsy, Hippocrates declared that the disease was but a natural illness like all others with a bodily cause. Contesting the prevailing notion that epilepsy was a "sacred disease," he pronounced such beliefs ignorant superstition. "For my own part," he wrote, "I do not believe that the human body is ever befouled by a God."

The writings of Hippocrates and his students and followers comprise the first records of thoughtful attempts to discuss mental illness on a medical basis. Hippocrates was the first man to seriously promote the idea that mental illness was the concern of the physician rather than the priest and the first to recognize the brain ("the interpreter of consciousness") as the most vital organ and as the source of emotion. "Man ought to know that from the brain and from the brain only arise our pleasures, joys, laughter and jests as well as our sorrows, pain, grief and tears: that through it we think, hear, see, and distinguish the ugly from the beautiful, the bad from the good, the pleasant from the unpleasant ... It is the brain which makes us mad or delirious, and inspires us with dread and fear, whether by night or day; brings sleeplessness, mistakes, anxieties, absent mindedness, acts that are contrary to our normal habits. These things that we suffer all come from the brain, including madness."

Hippocrates observed and described types of mental disturbance recognized today as postpartum psychosis, hysteria, psychoneurotic phobia. He noted that mental problems could follow injury to the head or be brought on by severe cases of diseases such as malaria, tuberculosis, or dysentery, and that these conditions were of a different nature from the purely psychological diseases which he thought resulted from imbalance of the humors. He called mental disturbances that were accompanied by fever "phrenitis"—to distinguish them from mania and melancholy—and said their source was the diaphragm rather than the brain.

In Hippocrates' physiology, the *pneuma* or breath was the source of intellect. Moving from the mouth, the pneuma bathed the brain and all parts of the body. In cases of insanity an excess of bile sent a sudden rush of the humor to the brain, causing disruption of intellection and of mood.

Hippocrates' diagnosis of the causes of hysteria persisted until modern times. Hysteria, he said, was an aberration caused by wandering of the uterus (*hysteron*) from its proper position. Therefore, it was only found in women. When Sigmund Freud delivered a paper on hysteria in male patients he was greeted with jeers by the Viennese medical establishment of the 1890s because—as every physician knew—you couldn't have a case of hysteria if you didn't have a uterus. Freud was to treat hysteria by a method which became known as psychoanalysis. Hippocrates suggested fumigating the pelvis with vapors through a funnel placed in the vagina in an attempt to lure the uterus back into position. He suspected, almost two and a half millennia before Freud, that sexual repression might be involved in hysteria, and if the victim was single he unhesitatingly suggested marriage.

Although the anatomy and physiology the Greeks described and passed on to the Romans and to the Christian world is now entirely discredited, Hippocrates is still revered. He is perhaps most honored today for his lofty conception of the obligations and high moral standards demanded of the physician. The "Oath of Hippocrates" is still taken by all medical students who accept their M.D.

degrees vowing to "practice your art in uprightness and honor."

The Greek philosophers did not hesitate to challenge medical opinion on the subject of insanity. Plato felt that man became deranged when his "irrational soul" (the emotions) became separated from his "rational soul" (the intellect).

In his dialogue titled *Phaedrus* he speaks of insanity not as divine punishment but as divine gift. "Prophecy is a madness," he says, defining it as an "inspired madness." He speaks of the madness which enables poets and artists to create. This variety, he says, results from possession by the muses. There is "the madness of love, the greatest of heaven's blessings." For those afflicted with less desirable forms of madness the philosopher suggests participation in ritual purifications and mysteries, which will release them from their possession. At the orgiastic Corybantic religious rites he felt that sufferers, aroused by the dancing, music, and chanting, would be returned to health. "Unwholesome mania is driven out by beneficent mania, and in the end both kinds of mania are gone."

Aristotle, Plato's pupil, felt that bile was the central issue in discussing causes of insanity but he considered the temperature of the bile more important than the quantity, and he noted that particular symptoms of madness varied with degrees of heat or cold. To Aristotle the heart, not the brain, was the organ which controlled reason. The brain, he wrote, was simply the place where hot vapors from the chest were cooled and then returned to the heart. He had faith in participation in the ritual mysteries as a cure and he was particularly interested in the power of music on deranged men and women. Unlike the people of King Saul's kingdom, who esteemed the soothing effect of music on the troubled mind, Aristotle favored music for its ability to excite suppressed emotion, which could then be therapeutically released. One experienced catharsis of disturbing emotions through music in very much the same way as through watching and vicariously experiencing the events in a theatrical tragedy.

The Roman physicians adopted the theories and therapies of the Greeks with admiration. The official medical attitude toward the insane in the Roman Empire was outstandingly humane, although only a few members of the elite benefited by these pleasant treatments, which centered on warm baths, massages, music, rest, and rocking in swings and cradles. Most physicians accepted humoral explanations of all illness, although Asclepiades, who came to Rome from Asia Minor in the second century B.C., was one of the few to challenge the role of the vital fluids. Asclepiades was a proponent of the theory of Democritus, which stated that the human body contained a great number of atomic particles whirling about. If the spaces between the atoms became too small or too great, Democritus held, the result was illness of one sort or another. A good dose of hellebore would relax the atoms and restore their natural position. Asclepiades invented a suspended adult-sized cradle which was used to calm the insane and he also contrived many types of stimulating and soothing baths. He felt that mental patients should be kept in light rooms rather than dark cells, which was the more common practice. He laid out a course of proper diet and drink, of music therapy, massages, and exercise. He urged that care be taken to stimulate the patient to speak and think rationally. He was completely opposed to the Greek tradition of bleeding patients until they were weak, insisting that this might have been all right for the strong systems of the Greeks, but that the Romans were already weakened by their habits of debauchery.

Controversy about medical practice led to some extreme opinions. Another Roman physician, Cornelius Celsus, urged harsh methods of frightening the patients—such as dousings with cold water—to jolt the mind from one state to another. He urged the use of strong emetics, bloodletting, starving, keeping the patient in total darkness. He favored doses of medicinal opium to assist sleep. He was one of the first physicians to urge that the heads of mental patients be shaved and massaged with aromatic oils, a procedure which continued into the nineteenth century.

The Carthaginian physician Caelius Aurelianus, whose writings outlined his own theories and those of his eminent predecessor Soranus, took issue with all such practices, as well as the indiscriminate use of violent purgatives and large doses of alcohol—apparently also a widely accepted treatment. Aurelianus wrote that practitioners who rubbed the head with rose oil excited "the very organ they are trying to quiet down; they use cold applications, ignorant of how often this acts as an exciting agent." He felt that music might bring on agitation and convince the patient further that he was possessed of evil spirits. He stated that denying sexual relations to the insane resulted in further distress. He urged that patients be kept in a soothingly quiet, warm, and light room in which beds were fastened to the ground. He wanted all the mentally ill confined to the ground floor to avoid suicides by jumping from windows. He favored restricted family visits, passive exercises such as rocking, avoidance of drugs whenever possible—particularly opium, which he said caused "morbid torpor instead of good sleep." He suggested instead the sound of running water as a natural sedative.

Soranus's therapies included playacting, preparation and delivery of speeches before other patients, and personal interviews in which patients were encouraged to talk about themselves while the therapist suggested to them how much nicer it would be if they behaved reasonably rather than in an antisocial manner. Among the causes of insanity Soranus listed head injury, too much wine, too avid a pursuit of money or glory. He chided philosophers for thinking that they were the proper people to dictate remedies for insanity, saying that indulgence in philosophical speculation was itself one of the causes of derangement.

The greatest physician of Roman times was Galen, who lived in the second century A.D. Galen accepted the humoral theories of Hippocrates. He theorized that physical spirits, carried by the blood, became transformed into vital spirits by the veins and the heart and then determined psychological functions after distillation in the brain. It was his view that melancholy might result from either an excess of black bile in the whole body or in the brain, or from the rise of injurious vapors from the stomach to the head. He also described a form of melancholy which he thought was caused by poor diet. Like his Greek predecessor, Galen noted a relationship between hysteria and suppressed sexual instincts. He recommended sexual intercourse as a cure for the psychologically induced physical complaints of hysteric personalities.

Galen lived in an age when brutality was commonplace, and he became intensely concerned with man's ability to control his passions. He wrote of the fact that his mother, when angered, bit her servants—a practice he regarded with dismay, although not with surprise. His father seems to have been more moderate in his outbursts. The son commended him for waiting until his rage had subsided before having his servants beaten, and for his restraint in denying the urge to kick or bite. In his book, *On the Passions of the Soul*, he added his own interpretation to the teachings of the philosophers known as the Stoics on the subject of the mastery of the passions. The book can be viewed as an early work on preventive psychiatry in which instructions are given for the encouragement of emotional stability in growing children through graduated mental exercises.

Galen, like other emminent classical physicians, was a sensitive observer. It is possible to interpret many of his findings as data which, rediscovered, became significant in the history of modern therapies. Galen noted that certain chemicals could radically alter mood and intellection. He noted that the poisonous herb known as hemlock (like LSD) can produce symptoms of insanity and that wine (like tranquilizing drugs) can eliminate anxiety, and these observations confirmed his belief that mental illness had a basis in bodily function.

Galen's teachings about anatomy, which were based entirely on animal dissection, were accepted long after his errors became apparent to scientists of the sixteenth century. The humoral theory he espoused dominated medical thinking fifteen centuries after his death. And yet Galen's conviction that mental derangement was a disease and that its victims deserved sympathetic and gentle treatment was totally ineffective during all those years in protecting the insane from ignorant prejudice and the almost unbelievably cruel treatment they were to suffer.

4
The Middle Ages: Faith, Superstition, Exorcism

Traditionally the Middle Ages have been viewed as a vast stretch of time during which progress in virtually every area of life was halted. In the field of mental illness the period was one of retrogression. The scientific investigations of the Greeks and Romans, which remained influential in the early centuries of Christianity, lost favor. The writings of the Greek and Roman physicians, stored in libraries and monasteries, were captured by Moslem invaders or forgotten. In the theocratic Middle Ages mental illness ceased to be a concern of European physicians. Monks, exorcising priests, inquisitors, and judges became the authorities on the subject, and the causes, symptoms, and treatment of mental illness were analyzed in accordance with belief in the devil—and his insidious methods for corrupting man.

In the early Middle Ages the Christian injunction to love one another and to heal the sick had led to the establishment at monasteries of places of refuge for the ailing, the homeless, the indigent. Kindly monks welcomed to these early hospitals lepers, widows, orphans, starving beggars. But many centuries passed before their pious sentiments were extended to those whose illness was mental rather than physical. The dreaded evil spirits of ancient days became the devils of Christianity, and demented wanderers who were thought to be possessed by these supernatural beings were regarded with horror and revulsion. Because of belief in the persistence of the devil, most cases of insanity were considered incurable except—possibly—through exorcism or contact with holy relics.

Men and women who were insane or retarded were generally left at liberty as long as they caused no disturbance to others. They were remorselessly teased, stoned, and beaten by anyone they passed who chose to abuse them and often died of hunger, exposure, or accidents. Those who seemed to pose a threat to public safety or decorum were confined in dungeons where they were flogged as punishment for their foolishness and violence. Most people believed that flogging had therapeutic value. If the devil had taken up residence in a person's body, the body should be made as unpleasant a domicile as possible —and then perhaps he would depart. The obvious way to accomplish this aim was by beating, starving, sudden showers with icy water. Many observers noted beneficial results.

Because of the cruel treatment doled out so readily to the mentally ill, many afflicted men and women strayed from the towns to live alone in secluded woodland places, where they sheltered in caves, dressed in animal skins or were naked, grew long hair and beards, were visited by angels and demons in vivid hallucinations. Those who imagined themselves divine personages and who were so indiscreet as to mention the fact risked being put to death for blasphemy and heresy.

In the Moslem lands of the East a quite different attitude toward the insane prevailed. To the Moslems the insane were the beloved of Allah, and they were treated with kindness and with awe. The most famous case of mental illness in Persian literature occurs in the old Arab tale "Layla and Majnun." In the Middle East, as well as in western Europe, it was believed that great love could lead to madness—and such is the case in this tale.

It begins with two schoolchildren, Layla and Kais, who fall in love as they study the Koran together. As Kais grows older his love for Layla becomes such an obsession that his classmates dub him *majnun* or "madman." When Layla's parents refuse to permit her to marry Majnun because of an ancient family feud, the crazed lover wanders off into the desert where he rambles about, composing

The last meeting of Layla and Majnun. Leaf from the Khamsa of Nizami. Persian, 1548. Smithsonian Institution, Freer Gallery of Art, Washington, D.C.

love songs to Layla, fantasizing about his passion, communing with the animals. Years later, when the wealthy man to whom Layla's parents have given her in marriage dies, she is free to marry as she pleases. She seeks out Majnun and at their meeting both fall into swoons—a favorite scene of the miniature painters who illustrated manuscripts of the story. Alas, poor Majnun has become so totally deranged by his frustrated passion that he is now unable to relate to the actual person of the beloved. He wanders off again into the desert, lost in dreams and visions of love. Soon after Layla dies, and Majnun, hearing of the event, rushes to her tomb, on which he also falls in death.

The poets had their own theories, but the medical explanation of the tragic tale was obvious to Moslem physicians of the period, who agreed that unsatisfied love caused noxious damming up of sexual secretions and resultant overproduction of bile. The rise of poisonous vapors to the brain caused madness. If not treated medically, the condition was known to be fatal.

In contrast to the devil-fearing Christians, the Moslems treated the mentally ill with intelligent concern, with kindness, and with specific therapies which had, for the most part, originated in classical Greece and Rome. The Moslem warriors who conquered large portions of Africa, Asia Minor, and Europe took possession of ancient manuscripts as spoils of conquest. As the new custodians of ancient learning, the Moslems began to translate classical texts into Arabic and to study the science of Hippocrates and Galen. In the eighth century they established medical schools and asylums for the physically and mentally ill in Bagdad. In succeeding centuries similiar institutions were established in Damascus, Aleppo, Cairo, and Fez, and in a number of cities in Spain. European travelers wrote wondrous accounts of the pleasant treatment given to the insane in these hospitals.

Because there was no demonology in their thinking, the Arab physicians attempted to treat sufferers by medical means. They accepted the humoral theories of Greece and Rome and prescribed cathartics, rest, proper diet. They were renowned for their preparation of drugs, and particularly favored the opiates. Special baths were constructed to soothe agitated patients. Concerts took place in charming gardens where fountains played and different types of music were carefully selected for their supposed therapeutic effect on mental diseases.

The Arabs also practiced an early type of psychotherapy. They urged that doctors discuss a patient's fears with him and offer calming reason to counteract delusions. They favored such diversions as hunting, riding, walking; and for cases of erotomania, in which patients were obsessed with sexual fantasies, they recommended strenuous games of ball and frequent cold showers.

The great physician Rhazes, who lived in the ninth century, was chief of the hospital at Bagdad. He is reported to have written 226 medical books and was referred to as "the Arab Galen." He was firmly convinced of the therapeutic effect of good diet, proper baths, massages with oil, a change of climate, peaceful, pleasant surroundings, and frequent indulgence in the game of chess, which he felt brought reason back to those who had lost it.

Avicenna, who lived a century later, sought the seat of mental illness in the stomach, liver, and spleen. Avicenna was recognized as a child prodigy when, at the age of ten, he memorized the complete Koran, and he fulfilled his early promise with a brilliant medical career. Like other Arab physicians he approached problems of diagnosis and cure unhampered by belief in supernatural agencies. He seems to have been particularly adept at clever diagnoses and he related interesting case histories to his students. One of his successful cases was the cure of a melancholic young man. The famous doctor suspected lovesickness. He placed his fingers on the patient's wrist and read off a list of women's names. He then read off the names of provinces, towns, and streets. By changes in the patient's pulse rate he discovered the name of the young woman and the town in which she lived. His recommendation was marriage. The patient took his advice and was cured. In another instance he reported undertaking the treatment of a man who thought himself to be a cow. The patient walked like a cow and made very disturbing moos. Avicenna told the sick man that indeed he was a cow and that he was being ordered to eat heartily because the butcher was coming to slaughter him in the morning and was expecting a nice fat animal. The patient, according to Avicenna's case history, ate lustily and then ran from the hospital—and kept running, presumably restored to reason.

Since the Moslem physicians were forbidden by the Koran to perform dissections or to view the bodies of women, physical examination was limited to living male patients—and no anatomical discoveries were made. Their actual contributions to the advance of medical knowledge were few, but they were known for their careful observations of the clinical course of diseases, for their humane hospital treatment of the sick, and for their sophisticated knowledge of the preparation and use of medicinal herbs.

In the Christian world there was little interest in medicine, although some histories mention physicians concocting crude "remedies" for the treatment of physical or mental diseases. An Anglo-Saxon prescription for curing madness caused by possession was to pound and mix together such plants as bishopwort, henbane, and cropleek, to add ale and cathartic grains, and to moisten with holy water. After the mixture was let stand overnight, it was to be drunk out of a church bell and would, presumably, send the devil off on the run. Another course of treatment prescribed by Byzantine pharmacologists was designed to last for two years, with ever more imaginative potions ordered each day. One day the patient was to consume the bloody cloak left by a dead gladiator which had been burned to ashes and mixed with wine. Another day he might try the testicles of a young cock, swallowed down with milk. Another treatment was the dried excrement of a dog who had been given nothing to eat for a week. Most people believed that the moon affected illness and that medication was more likely to help if taken during a particular phase of the lunar cycle. There was no attempt to evaluate the success of these "medicines."

It is reasonable to assume that the only cures which worked were those based on faith. It was an age of faith, and pious folk sought the services of an exorcist or recommended a visit to a holy well or shrine for a sick member of the family. Travel was an extraordinary happening, and pilgrimages to distant holy places were great events, undertaken in a mood of high expectation and confidence in the ultimate success of the venture.

There was considerable faith in the curative influence of the springs and wells at which previous miracles had occurred. People with all types of illness—including the insane—were plunged into these waters with appropriate incantations. In some instances muscular attendants would dunk the patient repeatedly until he was exhausted. He was then brought to a nearby chapel and special prayers

were offered for his recovery. Visits to holy wells continued in England through the nineteenth century. Sir
Walter Scott's poem "Marmion" tells of one such well in
Perthshire, Scotland: "Then to St. Fillan's blessed well,/
Whose spring can frenzied dreams dispel,/And the crazed
brain restore . . ." At St. Fillan's patients were plunged into
the well three times and then left, bound hand and foot,
to lie in a chapel nearby. If the patient managed to free
himself from his bonds, there was hope for his recovery.
If he was found the next day still lying tied, the outlook
was poor. In the late eighteenth century, two hundred
men and women were still brought to St. Fillan's annually.

A visit to a shrine in which relics of the saints were
preserved was an even more common therapy in the late
Middle Ages. The custom continues and miraculous cures
of the faithful are still reported. The two shrines most
frequently visited by the sick today are that of Saint
Anne de Beaupre in Quebec and that of St. Bernadette at
Lourdes, where 2 million people a year seek spiritual
aid in overcoming illness at the spot in southern France
where the Virgin Mary once appeared to a young peasant
girl.

The Christians of the Middle Ages erected shrines dedicated to saints just as the Greeks and Romans had raised
holy temples to honor healing deities. Relics—bits of bone
or skin or even nail parings of saints, or splinters of wood
from the cross on which Jesus was crucified—were vener-
ated by devout sufferers. Belief in the curative powers of
such relics stemmed from the tales of the instantaneous
cures effected by the touch of Jesus, the disciples, and the
early Christian saints. Many of the relics so enshrined
had been brought back from the holy land by the Crusaders.

The most popular shrine specifically visited by people

with mental diseases was that of St. Dymphna in Gheel—a town in Belgium still famed for treatment of the insane. The origins of the shrine date from the sixth century. St. Dymphna was a young Irish princess, the daughter of a widower. As she reached young womanhood, she was tormented by the incestuous advances of her father. The maddened intemperate man pursued his daughter to the continent and seized and beheaded her at Gheel. She is said to be buried there, and many miracles were reported at the site. She was canonized in 1247. An infirmary devoted to the care of the mentally ill was established near the shrine in the late Middle Ages, but when it became overcrowded the boarding-out system, for which Gheel is still famous, was instituted. Mental patients who arrived from all countries in Europe were boarded with local farm families. Retarded children who were left in Gheel by their parents were given domestic work in households or jobs in the fields. In 1852 the colony was taken over by the government and placed under the direction of medical administrators. Most patients still board with families today although a modern hospital is the central treatment area.

Faith healing continued as the only genuinely effective form of therapy during the Middle Ages—and this was to be the case in regard to mental illness until the nineteenth century. In the late Middle Ages, people reputed to have a healing touch achieved considerable celebrity. For several centuries, starting with Edward the Confessor in the eleventh century, the English kings were thought to have the power of curing by laying on of the hands, and they obligingly "touched" great numbers of sufferers on specified occasions. When belief in this power as an attribute of kingship died out, lay healers took over. They can still be found in all countries today.

The first lay healer to achieve fame was a fourteenth-century clerk named Valentine Greatrakes who became known as "the Irish Stroaker." Greatrakes did not silently touch the brow. His healing technique was vigorous and dramatic. While stroking and massaging the head of a sufferer he cried out, "God Almighty heal and strengthen you for Jesus' sake," in a great rich bellow. He received considerable acclaim for his ability to cure "falling sickness" (epilepsy) and possession. In recognizing and acting upon his intuition that he had the ability to heal, he became the first man of whom we have historical account to insist that divine healing could be accomplished not only by saints and kings and bishops, but by an ordinary mortal with special gifts but without particular learning or training.

In the late Middle Ages faith, which directed the sick to healers and to shrines, also led to outbreaks of bizarre group psychosis or mass hysteria. Historians refer to these strange occurrences as the flagellationist movement and the dance manias of the thirteenth, fourteenth, and fifteenth centuries. In an atmosphere of impending calamity, obsession with visions of the coming end of the world, and consequent fear of Hell, religious unrest led emotionally fragile people to outbursts of frenzied behavior over which the church had no control.

The members of the Brotherhood of Flagellants first marched through Europe doing public penance during the thirteenth century—the period of the Guelph-Ghibelline wars. Dressed in long robes with red crosses on their chests, they sang hymns as they walked, and when they reached a village, whipped themselves with long knotted leather lashes which were fitted with four iron prongs. The self-flagellation continued until the bodies of the penitents ran with blood. The flagellants were condemned by the papacy for their masochistic excesses and unseemly display of emotion and went underground, to emerge again at the time of the plague known as the Black Death. In this period of disease, famine, and increased fear of damnation they were again officially condemned, but to little avail. To the dismay of the Holy See, the flagellants —who were thought to be possessed—continued to demonstrate, marching and lashing themselves for periods of thirty-three and a half days according to a current ritual, announcing that flagellation was the only road to salvation, and seeking converts to their society as they went.

The dancing manias involved thousands of people who were seized with a compulsion to dance orgiastically, to laugh, sing, and leap until they fell from exhaustion. Contemporary reports indicate that dance manias took place in Cologne, in Metz, in Aachen, in Zurich, and in cities in France and in Flanders, involving in each case hundreds or over a thousand people. Today these mass happenings are often interpreted as having served as outlets for suppressed sexual and aggressive instincts. At the time observers were stunned with incomprehension and horror as men and women danced in churches and in the streets, jumping high in the air, calling out the names of demons, and explaining their acrobatics by insisting that they were dancing in a river of blood. According to several astounded eyewitnesses, who left records of the event, they clapped their hands, tossed their heads about, tore off their clothes in some instances, threw themselves on the ground, moved around convulsively on their backs, twitched, jerked, and in many cases, lost consciousness. It is reported of the dancers that some few were treated and cured by exorcism which, to medieval man, was the one reliable means of

The dancing mania. Engraving after a sketch by Pieter Brueghel. National Library of Medicine, Bethesda, Md.

attacking obvious cases of possession—whether of an individual or a member of an afflicted group.

All through the Middle Ages most cases of insanity were diagnosed as having been caused by possession by the devil and other evil spirits, although there was some limited recognition of other reasons for mental confusion—alcoholism, retardation, the delirium of fever, the ravages of old age. The idea of possession by demons had existed in ancient times, when exorcism—the ritual of commanding the spirit to leave the body of the possessed person—was often accomplished by such simple means as inserting a root into the nostril and drawing out the evil demon. In the Christian Era the rites of exorcism became infinitely more complex and formalized, although many paintings of the period still show the actual form of the demon emerging from the patient's nose or mouth. Medieval Catholic theology held that only reason separated man from beast and that the man who lost his reason lost his soul and would be eternally damned unless exorcism was attempted and successfully concluded. An illness caused by spirits could only be treated by a spiritual therapy. Healing by exorcism was performed by saints or bishops in the early centuries of Christianity, but in later periods lower-ranking clerics participated in the holy rites.

The possessed man or woman was thought to exhibit certain standard and recognizable symptoms. He reacted violently to images of the Savior or the sound of His name. He could not utter prayers and if he took the Eucharist he would promptly vomit. His face became altered, as did his voice. He appeared to others to be speaking in the tones of the evil spirit—and the words that came from his distorted mouth were curses and blasphemies. Often a gentle pious man or woman would speak a language no one had heard before or relate events he or she had not previously known. There were also more commonplace symptoms such as loss of appetite, feeling of great weakness, sexual impotence.

Against this violent derangement, the exorcist offered his most potent weapon—the name of God. He would bravely confront the possessed person, who often exhibited an unnatural physical strength, and try first to discover the name of the particular demon he was to exorcise. Asmodeus and Belial were the two thought to be most active. After offering prayers to reinforce his own spiritual peace and confidence, the exorcist would then assault the spirit, commanding him in the name of Jesus to return to the regions where he belonged, to leave the body of the possessed forever. A crucifix would be placed on the forehead and breast of the patient.

Catholic exorcism—conducted according to a ritual formalized in the seventeenth century—is still used today

St. Catherine Exorcising a Possessed Woman. *Painting by Girolamo de Benvenuto, 1470–1524. Courtesy of the Denver Art Museum, Denver, Colo.*

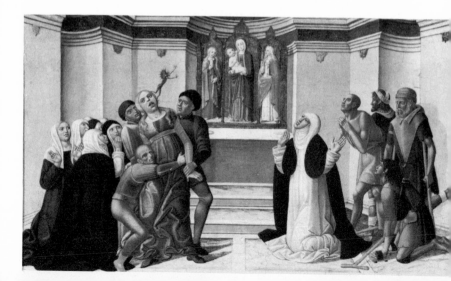

to a very limited extent. In the summer of 1976 criminal charges were brought against a Catholic bishop in West Germany after a twenty-two-year-old university student, who had refused to eat for some months, died of undernourishment while undergoing an extended exorcism which was recorded on forty-three cassette tapes.

Two surgical procedures for possession found some favor in the Middle Ages. Trephining, which had been a last-resort treatment thousands of years before the Christian Era, still had its advocates who drilled openings in the skull for the release of spirits. Outrageous charlatans known as "stone doctors" made an incision in the scalp and noisily dropped into a basin a stone they had palmed. Stone surgery seems to have been a subspecialty of the period and these performers also "removed stones" from other ailing areas of the body by the same method.

Insanity caused by alcoholism and intemperate living was diagnosed in the case of Charles VI of France who, at the end of the fourteenth century, became wildly paranoid and attacked his own men in a military encampment, announcing that he was being pursued by enemies. Because overindulgence in wine was blamed he was treated by prayers, rest, and mild diet and was restored to his senses. The king had a second incident of madness which was cured by a combination of spiritual aid and bed rest. Some of his followers went on pilgrimages in his behalf and he stayed home under the covers. The diagnosis was overindulgence and overexertion—and punishment by God for these faults. Later, when he was ill again, a wax figure representing him was sent to a shrine.

All through the Middle Ages it was considered indisputable that astrological forces—determined by the position of the heavenly bodies at the time of your birth—influenced your physical and mental health and that the moon had a special power over madmen. In the great Middle English poem by William Langman, *Piers Plowman*, we read of "lunatic lollers . . . mad as the moon sits." This belief seems to have had little relationship to prevailing demonological theories and can be traced back to pagan societies.

A thirteenth-century herbarium offers a specific cure "for lunatics who suffer from the course of the moon. If peony herb is bound on the neck of one who is moonstruck, quickly he will rise up healed; and if he carries it with him he will suffer no ill." A century later the cure was more drastic: "Incise the top of the head in the shape of a cross, and perforate the cranium so as to expel the noxious matter."

Only a few men of the late Middle Ages held deviant views on the causes of insanity. A monk named Bartholomew who lived in England in the late thirteenth century wrote a book on mental illness which was free of the demonological theories of the time. Bartholomew condemned not supernatural forces, but mental stress and overwork. He suggested that the agitated insane be kept isolated in dark silent rooms, bound hand and foot to avoid hurting themselves or others, and fed bread crumbs soaked in vinegar. He suggested soothing ointments and balms and cautious bleeding to promote healthful sleep, and for those who were not agitated he recommended some form of occupation and listening to music.

But most people viewed the madman as a hopelessly afflicted and highly undesirable citizen. At the very close of the Middle Ages a new means of protecting society from the ravings and ravages of the insane came into favor. Instead of simply being driven out of town, many were now put on ships. These vessels, with their cargo of demented men and women, sailed through the rivers and

Ship of Fools. Fifteenth-century woodcut. National Library of Medicine, Bethesda, Md.

canals of Europe. When the ships docked in foreign ports the natives gathered at the docks to enjoy the traveling circus. We do not know whether these floating jails overloaded with lost souls were designed simply for confinement of the insane or whether there might have been a higher motive, since water, the agent of purification, was considered therapeutic for the mad. Some think the ships might have been pilgrimage vessels, conveying the mad to shrines in other lands. It is likely that these pilgrims never saw home again once they had embarked. The metaphor of a sea journey as a search for one's soul or one's destiny has inspired a number of literary works, several of which have used the title Ship of Fools.

Setting the mad adrift may have seemed an ultimate cruelty to sensitive observers of the time, but the most drastic solution to the troublesome problem of dealing with the insane lay just ahead.

5
Witchcraft and Sorcery

It was during the Renaissance—the "rebirth" and the flowering of art, literature, science, and architecture, the age of geographical exploration and of exaltation of the individual and his role in an expanding universe—that treatment of the insane reached the ultimate limits of barbarism and horror.

In the year 1431 Joan of Arc was burned at the stake on charges of witchcraft. During the next three centuries an estimated three hundred thousand other innocent men and women were tortured and executed by the witch courts of the Inquisition. Although the purpose of the Inquisition was to stamp out heresy, vast numbers of the accused were guilty of only one crime, the crime of being mentally ill. In the Middle Ages a man or woman who raved about seeing or hearing spirits was generally judged to be possessed and in need of exorcism; in the fifteenth and sixteenth centuries the man or woman possessed by devils was judged a dangerous heretic. Driving out the devil was now accomplished by a newer, faster, and more certain method: burning his host. Although superstitions dating to earliest times hold that a possessed person can harm others, it was not until the period of the Inquisition that the mad-woman-witch-heretic was seen as a malevolent menacing being who could cause unspeakable disasters, including striking others mad, and who must be destroyed.

The Inquisition was a Catholic tribunal established in the thirteenth century and charged with the duty of wiping out heresy. In a number of European countries over the next four hundred years heresy was fought ruthlessly by religious and civil authorities. Although in earlier times heresy had been combatted by verbal persuasion, during the Inquisition period punishments ranged from fines to torture and execution. The condemned were permitted no defense before Inquisitorial juries. The special witch courts sought to identify "witches" (female) and "sorcerers" (male), who were alleged to be conspiring with Satan to carry forth his evil work on earth. Although they originated with the Catholic clerics of the Inquisition, they were continued with equal ardor after the Reformation by Protestants in England and Germany and the colony of Massachusetts.

The witch trials took place against a background of great ambivalence in medical thinking. Old superstitions about the causes of physical and mental illness persisted in the minds of the general population, but by the late Middle Ages students, physicians, and philosophers were immersed in the study of the writings of the Greek and Roman authorities. There was renewed interest in examining mental illness as a disease. Ancient manuscripts, brought back from Moslem libraries as spoils of the Crusades, were now being rediscovered. Interest in higher education had started burgeoning as early as the thirteenth century, and between the years 1200 and 1350 fifteen universities had been founded in western European cities. In the mid-

thirteenth century the German king Frederick II set up
an academic course of study for medical students which
bears striking similarities to contemporary programs. He
decreed that a doctor must study five years in a university,
spend one year as apprentice to a practicing physician or
in a hospital, and then take qualifying examinations.
Frederick also made certain that one human cadaver
would be dissected every three years for the education of
the faculty and all the students. His interest in science,
however, did not interfere with his conviction that insane
men and women who confessed to witchcraft should be
burned.

On all fronts interest in medicine as science conflicted
with primitive beliefs and superstitions. Astrology and
medicine were still closely bound at this time, and few
physicians would consider instituting treatment without
regard to heavenly signs. A famous fourteenth-century
surgeon, Guy de Chauliac, found trephining highly therapeutic in many cases of insanity but warned that it should
never be undertaken during the time of the full moon.
The progressive physicians of the late Middle Ages attempted to reconcile the classical humoral theory of the
causes of mental illness with the current belief in demonology. Arnauld of Villanova, an ardent Galenite, decided
that, since the devil enjoys a warm place, he is likely to
invade a victim in whom warm humors are prevalent due
to an excess of bile. The eating of wolf's flesh was recommended by other learned men as a cure for hallucinations,
particularly if the problem was "devil-sickness." Another
cure for the same ailment was a good beating with a whip
made of porpoise skin. Dunking in holy wells remained
popular.

By the mid-fifteenth century the humanistic writings
of Greece and Rome were being disseminated to an in-

creasingly literate populace through the means of the new invention, the printing press. Even though naturalistic explanations of mental illness were now widely available, few people questioned the proceedings of the inquisitors. The instinct for self-preservation undoubtedly kept some would-be dissenters silenced—any opposition to the establishment could be deemed heresy, which was punished by death—but there is compelling evidence that belief in witches and the harm they could perpetrate was widespread at all levels of society.

By the late Middle Ages the distinction between a mentally ill person and a heretic had become increasingly obscure. By the mid-fifteenth century, all mentally ill men and women were vulnerable to a charge of heresy. The inquisitorial finger pointed at eccentric old women, at demented housewives, at men who muttered as they walked—and accused them of perpetrating the work of the devil. The finger pointed, in a very high majority of cases, at women. Sex was seen as degrading to man, and woman, it was believed, had been plotting with the devil since the time of Eve, to seduce and destroy him. There were no questions asked when the English king Henry VIII, who had tired of his wife Anne Boleyn, accused her of witchcraft, saying she used her magical spells to seduce him. He cited as evidence of her alliance with the devil the fact that the marriage had produced no male heirs. Anne Boleyn was duly executed. In the atmosphere of this prevailing view of the relationship of the sexes, psychotic women voiced sexual fantasies and impious thoughts, "confessed" to cohabiting with devils and to plotting to harm others. If they didn't confess at once most of them did eventually—after being subjected to the cruelest physical tortures ever devised. Those who were sane and were accused of witchcraft confessed as well, although perhaps less readily. Some men were deemed sorcerers and were duly executed, but the fact that Jesus had been a man gave them an undisputable status that women lacked.

The *Malleus Maleficarum*, the handbook of the witch courts written by two Domonican monks of the fifteenth century, told how to identify, examine, and sentence a witch. The devil, said the pious monks, seeks always to lure man into sin. He does so by sending an incubus or succubus forth to cohabit with a human woman or (less

Burning of an insane woman during the sixteenth century. The Bettmann Archive.

often) a man, to confirm the pact to spread the devil's evil on earth. The incubi were male spirits, the succubi female spirits, and they were allegedly able to assume human form for their carnal purpose. Once the pact was sealed, the powers of the witch or sorcerer were limitless. According to the authors, Kraemer and Sprenger, witches could injure people in various ways. They could cause a man to have "evil love" for a woman or vice versa. They could bring about hatred or jealousy. They could cause sexual impotence. They could bring about bodily diseases, cause insanity, cause death. Any family in which illness or death occurred was entitled to point to a suspected witch (often the nearest eccentric or psychotic woman) as the cause of the problem. Witches were also blamed for the death or disease of animals, the drying up of milk cows, problems with crops. There were repetitive assurances all through the *Malleus Maleficarum* that women are inferior by nature, vice-ridden, impure, and vicious—and the obvious tools of the devil.

The search for "witches' marks" to assist in identification of the devil's cohorts was a degrading and invariably successful form of examination. The *Malleus* informed judges that the devil always kisses his subject to sign the pact—often in some private place. Therefore, the accused would be shaved of all bodily hair and brought naked before the inquisitors. At all times the witch was led into the court walking backward so that she would not be able to bewitch the judge. Any skin lesion—a birthmark, mole, or scar—could be pointed out as the spot on which the accused had been marked by the devil. Often, wrote Kraemer and Sprenger, the devil put his brand "in secret places, as among the hair of the head or eyebrows, within the lips, under the arm-pits and in the most secret places of the body." If no mark was found after a very thorough examination the accused would be pricked. It was written that the devil might leave an *invisible* mark—a place on the body which was insensitive to pain. The spot was located by pricking with pins and needles on all parts of the body. It is known today that hysterics often have areas of insensitivity of the skin and the test was quite appropriate for confirming this condition.

The witch courts insisted on confession—and since confession brought death, various means of torture were often found necessary. One handy device was the witches' collar—an iron collar with a metal tongue which went into the mouth and had a number of sharp prongs which pierced the palate, the tongue, and the inside of the mouth. This device was inserted and the witch was then tied to a post for twenty-four hours before being asked to confess.

Torture of witches and sorcerers was described as a means of driving the demon from the subject's body until he came forth to announce his defeat by the tormentors. Means of inflicting pain other than the witches' collar included simple immersion in ice cold water or use of such instruments as the Spanish boot, which crushed the bones of the foot, the rack or the "Catherine's Wheel," on which the body was stretched and torn, and many other imaginative devices conceived by sadistic minds.

How educated people of the period permitted such conditions to continue is difficult to imagine today. And yet, the burnings went on through generation after generation. God-fearing men and women who suffered some deprivation or illness continued to accuse others of having bewitched them, and inquisitors continued to condemn innocent people to horrible deaths. A few enlightened men of the sixteenth and seventeenth centuries spoke out. Paracelsus, an early sixteenth-century professor of medi-

cine, took a stand against demonology, saying, "Nature is
the sole origin of diseases." Johann Weyer of the Rhine-
land said that witches were sick innocent people and
that their torturers should be punished. He assured listeners
and readers that the devil simply could not engage in sexual
intercourse with human beings and that women who said
they had had such exotic experiences were simply mentally
ill or misguided people who had a great need to feel important. His book *De Praestigus Daemonum* is considered
a landmark in the history of psychiatry—and was listed
on the church's *Index Librorum Prohibitorum* until the
early twentieth century. Cornelius Agrippa wrote a treatise "On the Nobility and Pre-eminence of the Feminine
Sex" and one day in Metz ran the risk of execution when
he liberated a woman who had been accused of witchcraft.

In the seventeenth century, as the witch-hunt fever was
dying out in Europe, a number of group "bewitchments"
occurred in convents. The most celebrated case took place
at the convent of Loudun in 1632 when Soeur Jeanne des
Anges developed an erotic fascination with Urbain Grandier, handsome curé of a church in the town. When she
asked him to hear her confessions, the curé refused, saying
his responsibility was for the townspeople and not the
members of the convent. Soon after Soeur Jeanne des
Anges became ill. She claimed that demons had possessed
her because Grandier, who had a pact with the devil, had
sent evil spirits to incite her with an unholy love. She
was first treated by exorcism and for some months appeared
well. But soon her symptoms reappeared. She suffered
from forbidden sexual fantasies and during Communion
she threw the host into the face of the priest. Soon other
young women in the convent also spoke up. Urbain was a
wizard, they said, and he had caused pure women to experience carnal lust and to feel tempted to relinquish their

chastity and break their holy vows. Urbain Grandier was seized, tortured, and pressed to confess. On his way to the pyre where he was to be burned he was carried bound on a cart because his legs had been broken. When the monks walking alongside the cart struck him on the face with a crucifix he turned his head to one side. At last, the needed proof was given. The priest had rejected the image of Christ. Grandier was burned alive.

Reginald Scot, author of *Discoverie of Witchcraft*, wrote, at the end of the sixteenth century, "The common people have been so assotted and bewitched, with whatsoever poets have feigned of witchcraft, either in earnest, in jest, or else in delusion ... that they think it is heresie to doubt in anie part of the matter; speciallie because they find this word witchcraft expressed in the scriptures." He found no problem in imagining rational explanations for the experiences of the witches who confessed, and without the slightest fear he gave a few examples to support one of his assumptions—that the clergy themselves invented the incubus as a scapegoat for their own lechery. He wrote of a woman who reported that one night an incubus came to her bed and made "hot loove into hir." When she called out in alarm, Bishop Sylvanus was found under the bed by those who came to her aid. It was explained that the incubus had taken the form of the good bishop. Scot expressed grave doubt about the matter.

The witch trials were also condemned by the French essayist Montaigne, who saw the inquisitors as sadistic fanatics and the so-called witches as mental defectives, thoroughly insane, or hysterics who were highly susceptible to suggestion. In a broader sense, the witch trials can be viewed as the most far-reaching legally sanctioned method for destroying undesirables. The feared, hated, and burdensome insane were particularly vulnerable.

6
Trials and Treatments in Colonial America

The freedom-loving colonists who arrived on our shores in the early seventeenth century brought with them their hopes, their fears, their sociological and religious opinions. Although they had fled prejudice and mistreatment themselves they had as little concern about the rights of the mentally ill as their former oppressors. In the countries they had left, witch trials were still treating many of the insane by means of the pyre, while other mentally ill men and women were tossed into prisons or cellars to live out tormented lives in appalling conditions of neglect. Harmless indigent beggars who were withdrawn, depressed, and deluded still wandered through towns and on country roads. The same conditions prevailed in colonial America, where the insane were thought to be either in cahoots with the devil or depraved beings who had been afflicted by the deity as punishment for sin. They were judged inferior specimens, people to be despised—or at best, avoided and ignored. Their condition was considered, by virtually everyone, to be incurable, and therefore no public funds were allotted for any sort of medical treatment.

A number of observations had been made in Europe in

the sixteenth and seventeenth centuries, which demonstrated a rising spirit of scientific inquiry. Felix Plater, who like most sixteenth-century physicians believed that madness was caused by devils, spent long periods of time voluntarily living with deranged people who had been cofined to dungeons. He made astute observations of the symptoms and course of their illnesses and left a useful classification of various types of mental disorders. Charles Lepois observed that men as well as women suffered from hysteria and disputed the Greek view that the seat of the disurbance must be the uterus. Lepois was of the revolutionary opinion that the problem was in the head rather than in the reproductive organs, an observation that would be made at intervals through history—and vehemently opposed every time. In the seventeenth and eighteenth centuries other observers noted that mental illness often followed closely upon childbirth and that melancholia and mania can alternate in a given individual and might, in some instances, be forms of the same disease. Scientists also made note of the fact that some mentally ill patients recovered after suffering a high fever from a physical illness.

These findings had far-reaching significance in the history of medicine and little effect on the average layman, physician, or judge in Europe or in the American colonies. Physicians still preached the old Graeco-Roman humoral theories and few comprehended the significance of Andreas Vesalius's findings from the dissection of human cadavers which disproved Galen's notions. If they had been made aware of the fact that the new science conflicted with the old, they would have voted quite readily for the wisdom of the ancients.

The most popular book on mental illness—widely read in Europe and in America—was Robert Burton's rambling anecdotal *Anatomy of Melancholy*, published in 1621. Burton was not a physician but a dean of divinity at Oxford and a classicist. He listed psychological and social causes for insanity, including jealousy, fear, solitude, unrequited love, excess of religious fervor. He prescribed herbs, chess, music, physical exercise, travel, purgatives, a moderate sex life, and cathartic talks about the distress caused by depression with a friend or physician—"for grief concealed strangles the soul."

The level of medical practice in the American colonies was extraordinarily low. Since there were no medical schools until 1765, when the first—Philadelphia College (now the University of Pennsylvania)—was founded in Philadelphia, new generations of doctors learned as apprentices to older men, who passed on strange and primitive cures. Some physicians urged that a linen bag filled with bachelor's buttons should be worn around the neck at the wane of the moon to ward off madness. Others suggested a quilted cap filled with aromatic spices, or blistering the back of the neck, the top of the head, or the fingers and toes. Some doctors recommended an herb called St. John's wort, others a medication of crab's eyes, while still others favored earthworms or dog lice mixed with a bit of human perspiration or saliva. Frog's spawn was considered curative.

It was perhaps just as well for the mentally ill that most of the afflicted received no medical attention whatsoever. The young apprentice physician who considered treating insanity could learn from his esteemed teacher that Hippocrates believed in bleeding and purging—and he might also find in his European medical books some new treatments, such as "spirit of skull," which was thought to be particularly helpful if the patient also had epileptic seizures.

This preparation could be made only from the moss which grew on the skull of a man who had been killed or who had died in a violent accident. A preparation of spirit of skull mixed with wine was given to King Charles II of England in 1685 when he lay dying, but there is no evidence that it helped his condition.

Bleeding was tried for virtually any ailment, usually with careful attention to the phase of the moon. It was accomplished with knives and needles or leeches and left the patient weak, more manageable, and presumably improved. Due to a shortage of doctors in the sparsely populated new land, plantation owners, clergymen of all sects, and barbers became adept at bloodletting, and these untrained healers often concocted their own medicines and magical remedies as well.

One recorded case of a cure for madness involved a long-distance diagnosis. A messenger was sent to fetch a doctor and bring him to the bedside of a man many miles away who was having hallucinations. When the doctor learned that the patient also had a problem with one of his legs, the diagnosis was clear. He told the messenger that vapors rising from the infected leg had disturbed the man's brain and caused a problem in his eyes, which accounted for his hallucinations. The doctor entrusted the messenger with a vial of eyewash and another of strong brandy. His directions were that the patient wash his eyes and also have a drink every fifteen minutes until cured. His own presence would hardly be necessary. The case is reported to have ended successfully.

Although trials for witchcraft were becoming less common in England and on the continent, belief in witchcraft was still virtually universal. The famous Salem witchcraft trials resulted in the deaths of nineteen local citizens. In the American colonies hanging was considered the most humane form of capital punishment, and old-fangled European methods of execution such as burning and beheading were thought barbaric and repugnant. An observer at the trials named Thomas Brattle wrote a letter to a clergyman, insisting that many of the accused brought before the court were "known to be distracted, crazed women . . . unfitt to be evidences either against themselves or any one else." Others must have been aware of the facts, but it was not until after the irreversible tragedy had occurred that questions were raised. Soon after the hangings people began to wonder if indeed justice had been done. The twelve jurymen and one of the original accusers confessed to having been under a general delusion and no further executions for witchcraft ever occurred in this country.

As the old demonological explanations of the causes of mental illness became less commonly accepted, the medical practices of the Greeks were tried on the minority of the mentally ill who received any treatment at all. Families who assumed the affliction was hopeless locked up ailing relatives in closed rooms or in small outbuildings. A record from Pennsylvania dated 1676 contains the appeal of a penniless man whose son had become "quyt madd" for funds to help him build a "little block house" in which to confine the boy. A Massachusetts man also requested public funds to build a seven-by-five-foot hut in which he might lock his distracted sister. Needless to say, these coops were unheated and had no sanitary facilities whatsoever. It was accepted as fact that the insane did not feel the cold or the heat or object to filth or a near-starvation diet. In the absence of a social welfare system indigent people who became deranged and had no responsible relatives were either thrown into jail, beaten and chased out of town, or occasionally hanged. It was not uncommon for the officials of a community to auction off a madman to someone who would house and feed him in exchange for labor and free the community of responsibility for his care.

Early colonial legislation reflected the Elizabethan Poor Laws of 1601, which made local communities responsible for their own indigents. As a result, in many of the colonies, mad paupers who had been driven from town and who then returned were publicly whipped before being driven out once more. To be eligible for public funds, an indigent had to have resided in a locality for a given number of months. The stated period differed from one place to another and might be as long as a year. Newcomers to town were scrutinized with care, and if someone appeared likely to become a public charge, he was evicted before he had fulfilled residency requirements. Records show that the least desirable of all new arrivals were "Indian stragglers and crazy persons." In many cases demented people who actually had fulfilled the requirements for public relief were smuggled out of the town or county by night and left in some unfamiliar place to make out as best they could. As late as the 1860s a story was told of a Civil War widow who became crazed from grief, wandered the town in a distracted state, and slept on the graves of her two dead infants. When she told a local justice that she kept hearing her husband calling to her from the beyond, the keeper of the peace suggested that he might be waiting for her in distant Chicago. With public funds he purchased a ticket and hustled the deranged woman onto the train—and rid his town of one more nuisance.

Not all local officials were so unscrupulous. In several colonies it was general practice to house the indigent insane with private individuals at public expense. An early record from the Connecticut colony tells of a woman who claimed to be from Pennsylvania but who was found wandering about the town of Wallingford totally nude and thoroughly confused. The General Assembly of the colony ordered the town's selectmen to clothe the woman and find a home in which she could live and do some form of light work. The Assembly undertook to pay the difference between her earnings and the cost of her keep.

By the early eighteenth century jails and workhouses had been constructed in most of the colonies. The first almshouse was built in 1662 in Boston as a catch-all institution for petty offenders, sick people, the poor, vagrants, and other undesirables, including the mentally deranged. Many enlightened citizens objected to the mixing of the sick and the well, the lawbreakers and the virtuous poor, and a number of ill-fated attempts were made to arouse public interest in building separate facilities. John Hancock's uncle, Thomas Hancock, gave the city of Boston six hundred pounds toward building an asylum for "such unhappy persons as it shall please God in his Providence to deprive of their reason," but there was insufficient response to a fund-raising effort to add to the sum. Connecticut built an almshouse in 1727 to confine criminals, vagabonds, fortune-tellers, runaways, prostitutes, drunkards, and "persons under distraction unfit to go at large, whose friends do not take care for their safe confinement." The indigent insane who proved troublesome were now confined to the new jails and workhosues where custodial care of the most basic type was provided.

It was due to the humane views of a group of Philadelphia Quakers that the first general hospital was built in 1751. The petition for the hospital was written by Benjamin Franklin and signed by thirty-three concerned citizens of Philadelphia. One of the noble aims was "the Cure of Lunaticks," and the hospital became the first institution in America where the mentally ill were not viewed as criminals or sinners but as sick patients in need of treatment. A relative of the patient could have him or her committed by obtaining the signature of any physician and this was so easily obtained that there were undoubtedly abuses. Once admitted, the patient would be bled and purged and blistered. If he was less than peaceable and cooperative he would be put in ankle irons attached to the floor or in a "madd-shirt," an early type of straitjacket which was a simple cylinder of strong canvas reaching from neck to knees, pinning the arms against the sides.

Although standard medical treatment of the time sounds harsh today, the care of the insane at the Pennsylvania Hospital was motivated by large-spirited concern and a new optimism about the possibility of recovery. This hopefulness was related to the general spirit of enlightenment rather than to any medical discovery. If the patient was able to perform light duties, he or she was set to spinning or manual labor of some sort—not to earn keep but as a form of therapy. One of the hospital's less commendable features was that like the notorious "Bedlam" Hospital in London, where one hundred thousand visitors a year paid a penny to jeer at the maniacs, the Pennsylvania Hospital's "lunatick wing" became a famous local attraction. Philadelphians entertained out-of-town guests by taking them to the hospital, paying an admission fee of four pence, and passing the afternoon teasing, baiting, and staring at the madmen through cell windows. This practice continued until at least the third decade of the nineteenth century.

The first asylum in America built solely for the care of

the mentally ill was constructed in 1773 in Williamsburg, Virginia. For fifty years it was the only such institution in this country.

A young man who would later become known as "the first American psychiatrist" became a professor at the country's new medical school in 1769, at the age of twenty-four. Benjamin Rush, a Philadelphia Quaker and signer of the Declaration of Independence, was a man of liberal principles and of broad education. He was an active member of the first prison reform society in this country, which achieved virtual elimination of the death penalty in Pennsylvania. He was also an early advocate of higher education for women and of free public schools. He was enthusias-

The first mental hospital in America, at Williamsburg, Virginia. American Psychiatric Association Archives.

tically opposed to alcohol and tobacco, which he thought harmful to both health and morality. A passionate abolitionist, he founded the Pennsylvania Society for the Abolition of Slavery and the Relief of Free Negroes Unlawfully Held in Bondage.

Rush had graduated from Princeton (then called New Jersey College) before his fifteenth birthday. In his twenties he studied medicine at the University of Edinburgh medical school. Soon after he began practice he realized that his primary scientific interest was in the treatment of the mentally ill, whom he divided into two broad groups: those who suffered general intellectual derangement and those whose problem seemed only partial.

Many of Rush's methods, which were considered humane in his day, now sound very harsh. He bled his patients to an extraordinary degree, for which he received some criticism at the time and considerably more from practitioners of the next generation. Since he disapproved entirely of any restraint—chaining, whipping, or even madd-shirts or straitjackets—he had his own methods of keeping control. He invented a "tranquilizing chair" in which unruly patients were restrained for long periods of time. The chair, which held arms, legs, body, and head in a state of total immobility, was intended to heal through lowering the pulse and relaxing the muscles. Another device he valued, which had been invented by Erasmus Darwin, grandfather of Charles, was the gyrator. It was a rather simple contraption—a board like a spoke on a wheel, to which the patient was strapped so that his head pointed outward. The board could then be rotated at very high speed, sending the blood rushing to the patient's head through centrifugal force and supposedly relieving the congested brain.

Benjamin Rush's
tranquilizing chair.
National Library of
Medicine, Bethesda, Md.

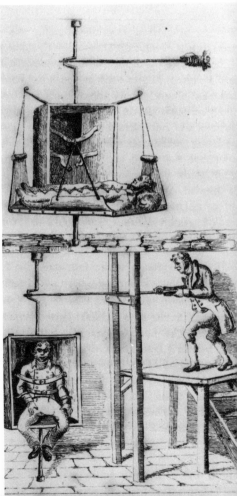

Circulating swing
and gyrator. National Library
of Medicine,
Bethesda, Md.

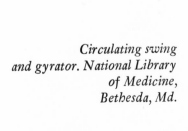

Rush believed that absolute control over patients was necessary—and that this control was best established by inspiring the patients with fear of the doctor's authority. The tranquilizing chair became a threat and a punishment, as did the twenty-minute ice cold shower. The kindly Quaker did not think it unseemly to subject patients to sudden dunkings by means of trapdoors over tubs or even to threaten to kill someone who needed a bit of terrorizing. He reported the case of a woman he cured after he threatened to drown her.

It is more heartening to know that Rush disagreed with current opinions that the insane, who were often left naked in dank cells all winter, were insensitive to heat and cold. He ordered comfortable cells, warm baths, exercise, amusement, mattresses and featherbeds instead of straw, and occupational therapy in the form of light pleasant work. He was anxious to see that the ill-paid sadistic attendants commonly found in hospitals and prisons were replaced with well-qualified kindly helpers. He urged patients to write diaries in which they analyzed the thoughts that troubled them, and then he had them read them and discuss them with him because he felt that repressed fears and desires were harmful. He also taught students methods of tricking patients into recovery, a kind of humane deception which Avicenna would have wholeheartedly endorsed. If a patient thinks she has swallowed a mouse, he said, give her medicine that she is told is a special mouse killer, or slip a mouse in the chamber pot after she has had a cathartic. He told of a patient who retained his urine because he had a peculiar delusion—until the day he told him the world was in flames and "nothing but his water would extinguish it."

Although many of Rush's methods of treatment fell

into disrepute in the nineteenth century, his work is of considerable historic importance, and he is held in great respect for his aims, if not for all of his actual accomplishments. In his book, *The Diseases of the Mind,* published in 1812, a year before his death, he decried "the slower progress of humanity in its efforts to relieve them [the insane] than any other class of the afflicted children of men." He welcomed the recent "humane revolution" which had started in France and England and the fact that the "clanking of chains and the noise of the whip are no longer heard in their cells," and he looked ahead with cautious optimism, warning that "much, however, remains to be done for their comfort and relief."

7
The Lunatic Asylum

"We let them, in chains, rot in their own excrement. Their fetters have eaten off the flesh of their bones and their emaciated pale faces look expectantly towards the graves which will end their misery and cover up our shamefulness."

So wrote a contemporary critic after visiting a European asylum in the late eighteenth century. When Americans built their first quarters for the insane in the Pennsylvania Hospital there were numerous long-established institutions in western Europe, and conditions in all but a few religious havens were horrifying.

The most famous of all mental hospitals was Bethlehem Hospital in London, known through most of its long history as "Bedlam." It was established in 1247 by a religious order and remained the only hospital in England until 1751. The original Bethlehem Hospital had confined "distraught and lunatik people" in a small stone building at Charing Cross near a number of leper houses. In the late fourteenth century the hospital was moved farther from the royal palace because the king complained of the noisy ravings of the inmates. Abusive treatment must have been the rule from the beginning. Records show that throughout the fifteenth, sixteenth, and seventeenth centuries, official visitors reported mismanagement and the harshest conditions imaginable. A 1598 inspection party found that the ward in which the insane were confined "was so loathesomely and filthily kept that it was not fit for any man to come into said house." By this point in its history Bedlam had already been taken over by the City of London and the first gawking visitors—who were less sensitive to shocking sights and less repelled by unseemly sounds and smells than the inspectors—were already flocking to the show. It was perhaps fear of losing this source of income that occasioned the inquiry.

During the sixteenth and seventeenth centuries men and women who were let out of Bedlam—and who presumably were not capable of making a living—were licensed to beg under a special royal poor law. They were provided with distinctive metal armbands as highly visible certification. Apparently some kindly housewives and farmers offered food and pennies because soon there were fake "Bedlam Beggars" with forged license bands on all the lanes and byways of Britain. The problem of imposters became so burdensome that in 1675 the license to beg was revoked.

Bedlam beggars appear in a number of Elizabethan and Jacobean plays. In Shakespeare's *King Lear*, Edgar, son and rightful heir of the Earl of Gloucester, escapes death by disguising himself as mad Tom o' Bedlam—"Poor Tom, that eats the swimming frog, the toad, the tadpole, the wallnewt and the water; that in the fury of his heart, when the foul fiend rages, eats cow-dung for sallets; swallows the old rat and the ditch-dog; drinks the green mantle of the standing pool; who is whipped from tithing to tithing..." William Shakespeare must have often seen the Bedlam beggars on the country roads leading to and from London.

Despite repeated investigations, by the seventeenth century conditions at Bedlam were, if anything, becoming worse. A journalist wrote, "It seems strange that any one should recover here. The cryings, screechings, roarings, brawlings, shaking of chaines, swearings, chaffings, are so many, so hideous, so great." There were recurrent reports of patients going without food of any sort for days

"Bethlam Royal Hospital," from The Rake's Progress. *Drawing by William Hogarth. National Library of Medicine, Bethesda, Md.*

on end because administrators had embezzled most of the
meager budget allowed for running the hospital.

The grim conditions in Bedlam were duplicated in most
of the hospitals for the custody of the insane which grew
up in such cities as Metz, Uppsala, Bergamo, and Florence
in the fourteenth and fifteenth centuries. In Spain a mental
patient was referred to as *un inocente*—a gullible childlike
person without malice. The mental hospital was called the
hospital de inocentes, and patients were treated in a relatively kindly fashion. In a number of European countries
the Order of the Hospitalers established general and mental
hospitals where patients participated in prayers and masses,
talked to the director each day about their problems, and
were never whipped or chained. Hospitals known for their
kindly treatment of the sick were also started by the Order
of St. Vincent de Paul in the late sixteenth and seventeenth
centuries. In 1566 the first mental hospital in the New
World opened in Mexico City.

Quite another type of shelter was built in France. In
1655 King Louis XIV established the Hôpital Général
in Paris, where the poor, mental defectives, cripples, abor-
tionists, blasphemers, delinquent children, and the insane
were herded under one roof and given minimal custodial
care. Four years after the all-purpose establishment was
built, six thousand wretched people were crowded within
its walls. Similar institutions were built in Germany and in
England. Society was protected at the least possible expense from the sight and sounds of the sick, the poor, the
helpless, and all other undesirables.

The mentally ill were housed in dungeonlike cells, often
in the basements of these institutions, and treated like sub-
human criminals who deserved punishment. They were
considered incurable and also totally insensible. In their
quarters there were no provisions for sanitation, heat, light,

ventilation. Cells were generally windowless and had heavy steel doors with small openings through which scraps of food were pushed at intervals. Attendants were picked from the lowest elements of society. They were hired for their physical strength and forbidding appearance and were equipped with bullwhips and given the right to restrain or punish patients as they saw fit. Most were barbarous and sadistic; many were former convicts, chosen not because they had been rehabilitated, but because of their aggressiveness.

A high percentage of the insane were confined not in hospitals or poorhouses but in jails. One observer described the often totally naked patients ranting in their damp airless dungeons. "Under such terrifying conditions, it would be easier for the most rational person to become insane than for a madman to regain his sanity," he wrote. Other people of conscience described the horrifying din made by the tormented inmates—"such a rattling of chains, drumming of doors, ranting, howling" that one anguished visitor could think only of the uproar of lost souls in Hell. It was commonly believed that the insane had extraordinary muscular strength and this view justified keeping people continuously chained year after year. In one institution in England it was reported that seventy of the four hundred patients had been in chains for twenty years or more.

Conditions fully as horrifying continued to prevail in places of confinement in Europe and in America well into the nineteenth century, despite the fact that the first half of the century was to be—for a minority of the mentally ill and their physicians—an age of great optimism, of humane and enlightened treatment, of exciting results in the form of high statistics on cures. The construction of "lunatic asylums" in state after state of the new republic in the 1820s, 30s, 40s, and 50s was greeted with excitement as evidence of social reform and advanced medical practice. After centuries of deepest pessimism, mental disease came to be viewed as a fascinating medical problem. Furthermore, for the first time in world history it was considered a medical condition which could, in almost all cases, be cured—if sufferers were treated in the therapeutic environment of the new model institutions. The "asylum" came to be viewed literally as a place of refuge, a setting in which the sick could find shelter from a harsh world and where they could mend.

The development of the model American lunatic asylums of the early nineteenth century was one result of the intense pressure for political and social freedom which had led to revolution in America and in France and which was to inspire reform movements of all sorts in the post-Revolutionary period. Antislavery sentiment and movements for penal reform were widespread among liberals and visionaries. There was considerable interest in the first attempts to educate the blind and the deaf. New communal living experiments were based on lofty Utopian ideals. A spirit of optimism and confidence in science and social reform was pervasive.

The most famous name in the history of reform of mental institutions was that of a Frenchman, Philippe Pinel. Born in 1745, the same year as Benjamin Rush, Pinel was the son and grandson of physicians. When a young friend became insane and committed suicide, Pinel dedicated himself to investigations into the problems of mental illness.

Although medical education in France at that time was still based on the teachings of Hippocrates and Galen, Pinel studied his patients' symptoms and behavior and became convinced that mental illness was not physical but psychological in origin, that it arose from emotional stresses and must be treated by psychological methods. In 1791 he visited the vast Bicêtre in Paris—a combination prison, hospital, and orphanage for male inmates of all ages—and he wrote a chilling condemnation. The following year he was appointed administrator of the institution and was urged to improve the conditions he so deplored.

Pinel was a truly liberal, sympathetic, and devoted physician. He is described as a shy, small man with a speech defect—who was intrepid in facing the most violent of his patients. The brutal treatment the inmates of Bicêtre had received had made many so frenzied that no one dared get near them. The insane were, at that time, routinely restrained with chains and fetters if they were at all un-manageable. To the alarm and astonishment of everyone, the new administrator unchained twelve of these patients. The first was a former military man who had been confined for almost forty years and who was feared by all the atten-dants because he had at one time killed a fellow patient with a blow from his manacles. When his chains were re-moved and his cell door opened, he was at first unable to rise to his feet. Soon he learned to walk again, stepped from his cell, and became a docile willing assistant in the institution. All in all Pinel liberated fifty-three of the chained inmates of the Bicêtre and each one became man-ageable. He had proven, to the satisfaction of many ob-servers, that patients became increasingly violent *because* they were so cruelly restrained. Two years later he left the Bicêtre to become head of the Salpêtrière, a similar institution for women, where he also began by releasing a great number of the patients from their leg irons and manacles.

Pinel was eager to relay to others the secret of his suc-cess. Although he removed physical restraints from his patients, he substituted another type of coercion, which was personal authority: "If [the patient is] met, however, by a force evidently and convincingly superior he submits without opposition or violence," Pinel wrote. In intractable cases, the patient was to be punished by brief confinement in a strait waistcoat or by being restricted in a dark room. In comparison to floggings and chains, these punishments were gentle indeed.

The precedent-shattering reformer had ample opportunity to confront his patients since he made daily rounds, took careful notes, and accumulated the first psychiatric case histories on record. In 1801 he published his *Medico-Philosophical Treatise on Insanity*, and the era of "moral treatment" was launched in a number of western European countries and in the new republic across the ocean.

The word "moral" did not, in psychiatric usage of the period, have the connotations of right and wrong that we associate with it today. "Moral therapy" was psychological therapy, as opposed to physical treatment. The causes of mental illness were seen by Pinel as predominantly psychiatric or "moral" stresses, and the therapy was aimed at increasing the patient's "morale"—his confidence in himself and expectation of being well. Moral treatment was compassionate treatment. It meant that the patient was to be encouraged to discuss his concerns and that his attention and interest were to be aroused by friendly, carefully directed conversation. He was not to be left idle but was to be kept occupied all day with purposeful activities. The patient was encouraged to develop self-control and self-esteem, to relearn these attitudes in the proper environment of a mental institution, where he was sheltered from the stresses of everyday life and his previous surroundings. Pinel opposed bloodletting, indiscriminate use of drugs, and all contrivances to shock, jostle, spin. He insisted that attendants must behave toward the patients with a kindly firmness and that no indignities in their treatment of the ill were to be tolerated. He prescribed a fixed and rigid routine of sleeping and eating and thought rural location for asylums more therapeutic than urban.

After studying hundreds of mental patients, Pinel concluded that there were four types of insanity, which he called melancholia, mania, dementia, and idiotism. As causes he listed strong passions and excesses first, and also intense studies and mental strivings, overwork, heredity, alcoholism, fever, head injuries, and an irregular mode of life. To Pinel social factors were the major source of distress, and isolation in the institution the only route to cure.

As Pinel sought to institute moral treatment in France, similar reforms were taking place in Italy, Germany, and particularly in England, where conditions were as distressing as they could possibly be. "There is hardly a parish in which may not be found some unfortunate creature, chained in the cellar or garret of a workhouse, fastened to the leg of a table, tied to the post in an outhouse, or perhaps shut up in an uninhabited ruin," wrote a concerned peer to the Home Secretary. Some, he noted, were "left to ramble half-naked or starved through the streets or highways, teased by the vulgar, ignorant and unfeeling, the scoff and jest of all." Those confined in hospitals suffered even greater hardships.

William Tuke, a Quaker layman, was aroused to action in his sixtieth year by observations of the inhumane treatment of the insane, and he dedicated the rest of his life to this concern. He established an asylum near York in the 1790s. The York Retreat, originally offering refuge only to members of the Society of Friends, was dedicated to kindly treatment of patients and lack of physical restraints. A visitor reported that patients were brought to the asylum "frantic and in irons" and that they were quickly released.

"By mild arguments and gentle arts they are reduced almost immediately to obedience and orderly behavior." He described the "government of humanity of consummate skill which requires no aid from the arm of violence and the exertions of brutal force." Patients were kept busy with domestic labor, manual and agricultural work, sports and recreational activities. Rooms were light, warm, well ventilated. There were books and games. When Tuke founded the York Retreat, he was unaware of Pinel's work in France.

In 1813 William Tuke's son Samuel published *A Description of the Retreat* and the reform movement was fully launched. In America and in Europe enlightened leaders eagerly accepted the optimistic enthusiasm of Pinel and Tuke about methods and cures. The House of Commons conducted inquiries into the scandalous conditions of hospitals in England. Across the ocean, new hospitals were constructed on the model of the York Retreat. The Hartford Retreat in Connecticut—one of the earliest mental institutions in the country—even adopted the name.

It is interesting to note that both in England and in America the harsh treatment given to a royal madman— King George III—was seen as shocking and discreditable. George III is now known to have been the victim of a very rare hereditary disease named porphyria, an incurable metabolic disorder causing such symptoms as persistent cough, acute pains in the chest and stomach, very fast pulse and fever, delirium with profuse sweating, severe insomnia, painful swelling of the limbs, inability to taste—and finally hallucinations and delusions. During his periods of madness, which became more severe after about 1810, the king became convinced that an oak tree in Windsor Park was his ally Frederick the Great of Prussia. He attacked the

Prince of Wales and violently tried to bang his head against a wall. He became a "flasher" and exposed his genitals to ladies of the court.

His physicians saw to it that he was bled and purged and straitjacketed, roughly gagged and strapped to the bed. Often a servant was instructed to sit on top of the king and keep him pinned. The royal patient's feet were blistered with Spanish fly and mustard plaster in an attempt to draw out "ill humors." Since he already suffered pains in the limbs from his disease, when the new irritation became infected he tossed in agonies and attempted to remove the plaster, but his doctors promptly put him in a straitjacket again. The king tried desperately at one time to make a getaway on horseback; he was chased by eight men and imprisoned for a month, constantly kept weak by excessive bleeding and strong doses of emetics. The fact that the king survived his medical treatment and lived to become virtually blind, totally deaf, lame, and demented beyond recall before he died at the age of eighty-one was remarkable, and perhaps his greatest misfortune.

By the year of his death, 1820, the first American asylum modeled on the York Retreat had been built in Frankfort, Pennsylvania. The Friends Asylum, which also, at first, admitted only Quakers, was founded by a Quaker philanthropist, as was New York's Bloomington Asylum in 1821. In 1818 the McLean Asylum was built in Massachusetts, and in 1824 the Hartford Retreat was opened. Next came Vermont's Brattleboro Retreat, built in 1836, and Rhode Island's Butler Hospital in 1847. The first state-supported institutions, in which care was more often custodial than therapeutic, were built in the 1820s in Kentucky, New York, Virginia, and South Carolina. The first state institution to offer moral treatment as practiced in the private and corporately owned hospitals was the Worcester

State Lunatic Asylum in Massachusetts. By 1860 twenty-eight of the thirty-three states would have public asylums for the insane and the total number of lunatic asylums in the country would be sixty-three.

Horace Mann, the famous educator, was, like most enlightened and idealistic Americans of the period, enormously enthusiastic about the new moral treatment. "The whole scheme of moral treatment," he wrote in 1833, "is embraced in a single idea—humanity—the law of love—the sympathy which appropriates another's consciousness of pain and makes it a personal relief from suffering whenever another's sufferings are relieved."

In the new asylums, patients—most of whom came from the middle and upper classes—were first divided into groups by their symptoms and the severity of their illness. It was believed that restraint led to violence and that idleness led to stagnation. All who could work were expected to put in three or more hours a day in the hospital or on the grounds. Patients were also encouraged to keep themselves occupied mentally with study, reading, discussion groups. They listened to music and to lectures, were frequently reevaluated and given increasing freedom from supervision as they improved. The hospital director and his family sat with the patients at meals and spoke to them as friends and companions. There was daily contact between the psychiatrist-director and each patient, including private and group discussions. Notes, case histories, and statistics were enthusiastically compiled, all attesting to the success of the new mode of treatment.

Charles Dickens visited the United States in 1824 and in his *American Notes* he describes his visit to the Boston Lunatic Asylum. He was particularly impressed by the warm relationship between the hospital supervisor and the patients, by the fact that patients were taken on carriage rides and other excursions, by the knives and forks offered at meals, by the weekly dances and the meetings at which patients participated in passing resolutions on hospital routines.

Statistics on cures which began to emanate from the new institutions generally related to recent acute cases. Insanity was considered almost entirely curable if the patient had been ill for less than a year. It was thought that the presence of mental illness brought about actual physical changes in the surface of the brain but that the brain was particularly malleable and successful psychological treatment would erase these distortions. If illness became chronic the brain became less flexible and less capable of being healed. Although autopsy reports failed to confirm this theory, it was felt that once sufficiently sophisticated techniques were evolved for studying the brain, the suspected flaws would be found. This explanation of the relationship between physical and psychological alterations in the brain remained unchallenged until after the Civil War.

As to the statistics that were greeted with such enthusiasm, they too were later reevaluated. One Dr. William Awl, who reported that 100 percent of his patients were cured, was dubbed "Dr. Cure-Awl." The eminent Friends Asylum was found to have committed the mathematic crime of counting as cured each patient who was discharged, even if he was subsequently readmitted several times. It was found that 87 persons accounted for 274 cures claimed by the asylum during the 1830s and 1840s. At Bloomingdale Asylum a woman who was admitted 59 times in a twenty-nine-year period was listed on discharge 46 times as "recovered."

In 1844 the country's leading psychiatrists, who were the administrators or "medical superintendents" of the major asylums practicing moral therapy, formed the Association of Medical Superintendents (now the American Psychiatric Association) and inaugurated a periodical called the *American Journal of Insanity* (now the *American Journal of Psychiatry*). The supervisors—in their journal and at their meetings—directed much of their attention to discussing the proper physical plan for a lunatic asylum. Unlike new European institutions, which were most often housed in older structures, the American asylums were built for the purpose and constructed according to the precepts of the new approach. Most popular was the wing design conceived by one supervisor of the Pennsylvania Hospital for the Insane, Dr. Thomas S. Kirkbride. It provided for accommodations for no more than 250 patients, a number agreed to be the maximum who could be appropriately treated in a single institution. The plan allowed for three sets of wings on either side of a central section housing the kitchen, offices, reception rooms, chapel, and an apartment for the supervisor and his family. Patients would be grouped in wards according to the severity of their disease. Great attention was given to providing good light, ventilation, and fireproofing. Each hospital was to have a minimum of one hundred acres of land for farming and for privacy. A number of Kirkbride buildings dating from the second half of the nineteenth century still stand, having undergone revisions, additions—and several changes in philosophy.

Dr. Amariah Brigham, supervisor of the State Lunatic Asylum at Utica, New York, had great confidence in the therapeutic benefit of challenging deranged people's intellects, and he instituted courses of study for his patients. The hardworking "students" became the subject of a humorous drawing in the asylum's patient-run magazine, *The Opal,* also conceived as a therapeutic project. This was not the only publication written and printed by patients in the asylums of the period. The *Retreat Gazette*, first issued in 1837 at the Hartford Retreat, bore a good-humored message from its editor, who hailed it as "something new under the sun. For although there are many newspapers that are crazy enough in all conscience, yet we

Cartoon from The Opal, *showing a patient at his studies. American Psychiatric Association Archives.*

know of none that acknowledge themselves to be so." The *Asylum Journal* of the Vermont Asylum for the Insane bore the motto, "We have all, at some time, been mad," and attempted to correct public views of insanity and explain modern methods of treatment.

The medical superintendents boasted of their innovations and successes. The supervisor at Bloomingdale Asylum claimed that his three-year course of lectures in such subjects as chemistry, astronomy, animal physiology, poetry recitation, and the history of Malta (accompanied by magic lantern slides) was enthusiastically attended. Dr. Samuel Woodward of the Worcester State Lunatic Asylum gave razor-sharp haying implements to four men who had been charged with homicides—and sent them happily off to work. The supervisor at another asylum reported that the institution ran like a "quiet and happy family, enjoying social intercourse, engaging in interesting and profitable employments, in reading, writing and amusements."

Unfortunately, only a fractional minority of the mentally ill were given access to the new approach to therapy. In 1841 a frail forty-year-old teacher in East Cambridge, Massachusetts, named Dorothea Lynde Dix volunteered to teach a Sunday School class for women prisoners. After class she walked curiously around the prison and found to her horror that a number of insane men and women were incarcerated there—kept in cold cells and given no medical or psychological treatment whatsoever. Although chains and whips were little in evidence, abusive treatment, filth, cold, and neglect were rampant. The passionate reformer spent the next two years on a personal investigation in which she discovered how many of the mentally ill in all states were deteriorating in dismal jails and almshouses.

Dorothea Dix, who like most progressive Americans had been impressed with the reports being issued from the new lunatic asylums, was horrified to find how few Americans were actually receiving the care offered in the comfortable new buildings. She became determined that the great numbers of insane poor must be moved to asylums where they would receive humane enlightened treatment and be given hope of recovery. During the next thirty years she approached state legislatures and local philanthropists with her pleas for funds to move the indigent insane to asylums. She crusaded in New England and then in Pennsylvania, Indiana, Illinois, Kentucky, Tennessee, Missouri, Mississippi, Louisiana, Alabama, South Carolina, and Maryland. Still fired with her cause, the reformer moved on to Nova Scotia and Newfoundland. She is credited with having exerted sufficient influence on legislators and donors to found more than thirty additional state institutions for the mentally ill.

What happened to end the era of moral therapy? Despite the fact that cure statistics of the 1820s through the 1850s were often grossly exaggerated, there is no doubt that a great many people *were* cured by the personalized care and encouraging environment of the best early asylums. But in the pre–Civil War period great changes took place in America which made the continuation of these programs impossible. Dorothea Dix's campaign, although motivated by the most honorable and estimable humanitarian concerns, brought thousands of indigent insane into small institutions, leading to rapid overcrowding. The arrival at the asylums of so many native-born paupers was augmented by a great influx of impoverished recent immigrants from Ireland who had become mentally ill. Increasing attention was paid to the fact that no one had proved brain lesions were caused by environmental pressures. There was a strong shift of opinion to the theory that insanity was determined by heredity, not by environment. Would a change in environment help someone who bore the seeds of his problems in his genes? psychiatrists asked. If not, why bother with improving the asylums?

The medical superintendents themselves began to question some of their most deeply held beliefs. Before the 1840s, few of them had been exposed to people who came from the lower economic, social, and educational levels. It had been thought that the upper classes, with their more demanding tastes, higher sensibilities, and greater desire for success, were more susceptible to insanity than the poor. Dorothea Dix was of the opinion that black slaves and American Indians lacked ambition and therefore were not threatened by insanity. Medical superintendent Edward Jarvis called insanity "the price we pay for civilization." There had even been a degree of national pride in the fact that the number of insane seemed to be increasing. It was said that in Europe, where sons simply follow in the same path as their fathers, there was less insanity than among the freedom-loving people striving ahead in the land of opportunity. But suddenly the institutions were crowded with indigents and insanity became less classy. In the minds of psychiatrists and the public it became related to poverty, alcoholism, vicious habits, moral corruption, incurability, hopelessness. Inevitably institutional neglect followed.

Prejudice against the Irish immigrants was very real. The 1854 and 1858 reports from the State Lunatic Asylum in Worcester, where many had become patients, referred to them as "coarse," "filthy," "rough," "unable to adapt to life in America." They were accused of crowding out the "intelligent yeomanry of Massachusetts who can afford to pay the cost of their board and will not ask for charity."

Some psychiatrists urged that Irish patients be transferred to state almshouses. Many wanted separate and definitely unequal facilities with less money allotted to the daily maintenance of the immigrants.

To add to the pessimism, the new European "theory of degeneration" suggested that insanity resulted from the "law of progressivity," by which each generation of an afflicted family became more unstable mentally. The first generation of such a family might simply exhibit nervousness, the second would be neurotic, the third psychotic. The next step was thought to be severe mental retardation and inability to reproduce.

Under the influence of these new attitudes the old cure rates which had seemed so exciting were reexamined and debunked. The use of physical restraints in mental hospitals became routine again. When visiting scientists from England noted the more common use of restraints here than abroad, superintendents assured them that restraints were necessary in this country since violence was evidence of a more democratic society. In England, they said, the poor were intimidated by their doctors, who were of superior class, but this was not so in America. As hospital populations increased, physicians made less and less attempt to continue personal interviews with patients. Because of acute overcrowding patients were observed to be sleeping in halls. The lunatic asylum lost its atmosphere of order, optimism, and progress.

In the post–Civil War period the influential superintendent of the Utica Lunatic Asylum, Dr. John Gray, insisted that only a physical disease could lead to insanity. He did not believe in psychological treatment but only in rest, careful diet, and good ventilation. He was particularly proud of the rotary fan he had invented for use in his hospital. Patients of the period wrote of cruel treatment

The Utica Crib. The Bettmann Archive.

at the asylum and many spoke of having been confined in the "Utica Crib"—a narrow bed with slatted sides and a slatted top which locked down in such a position that it was virtually impossible for the patient to turn over. "There is as much space between the patient's head and the lid as if he were in a coffin," one survivor wrote. The crib, it was alleged, was used as a restraint for the violent—and, at the will of the attendants, as punishment for the unsubmissive. Although patients at the Utica hospital claimed that the device had been invented there, it was apparently also used in other asylums.

When Charles Guiteau, the assassin of President Garfield, was on trial for his life, it was Dr. Gray who, because of his considerable reputation as an expert witness, was called to testify. Although Guiteau had exhibited flamboyant symptoms of irrationality, Gray stated that "crime and depravity" were not the same as insanity. Guiteau was hanged, and Gray's views as expressed at the trial were a strong influence in hindering future efforts at attaining psychological understanding of the behavior of the mentally ill. This pessimism about the curability of mental illness, which began in the 1850s, would last until after World War II.

In the 1860s and 1870s a number of cured mental patients wrote exposés, bringing to public attention the inhumane treatment they had received at the hands of sadistic attendants. Descriptions of harsh restraining devices, rancid food, arbitrary disciplinary methods, and total lack of activities planned for the patients brought shocked response from sympathetic readers. "On Ward's and Blackwell's Islands the insane sit day after day doing nothing. In all probability these two asylums are the worst in the civilized world. Scarcely anything is more injurious than to allow a lunatic to sit and brood over his condition. There is no large city in the world, not even excepting Constantinople, where there is such poor treatment of the insane as in New York," said an article in the *New York Herald* in November 1879. The report alleged that at Auburn Asylum a patient had been shot in the elbow by the superintendent, that patients were suspended by their wrists as punishment —in one case for fourteen days—and that they were frequently "paddled." The superintendent, the article said, carried a revolver with him at all times. The mattresses were full of vermin and the food was inedible. Although people who had been cured were not released, it was reported that a wealthy madman who had murdered someone before his confinement was let go—on provision that he settle in Europe and commit any further murders outside New York State.

In 1887 Nellie Bly, an intrepid young reporter for the *New York World*, accepted her editor's suggestion that she pose as a deranged person and have herself confined to the institution on Blackwell's Island. Under the alias of Nellie Brown ("so the initials would agree with my linen") she checked in at the Temporary Home for Females on Second Avenue, where she sat about looking depressed and telling all who would listen that she feared the other women in the hotel would murder her. Soon police arrived at the hotel, escorted her to the station, found physicians to certify her as insane, and she reached her destination. Her accounts of the inactivity, absence of hygienic amenities, lack of attention from the medical staff, rough treatment by sadistic nurses who scolded, screamed, and teased made fascinating reading on the front page of the newspaper for two weeks.

Public indignation was aroused and rearoused and would continue to be stirred by first-person accounts dating from Nellie Bly's exposé to Clifford Beers's autobiographical account of his three years in public and private institutions in Connecticut, *A Mind That Found Itself*, published in 1908. In the mid-twentieth century Mary Jane Ward's *The Snake Pit* took its title from the early practice of lowering the insane into a pit filled with snakes in the expectation that the shock might return them to sanity. The book, which was set in a mental institution, became a film and the combined success of novel and film led to the use of the term "snake pit" to describe an asylum. Again public awareness of prevailing conditions was aroused and impetus for change was given some very limited expression.

Although current researches in the history of psychiatry see the decades of moral treatment in America as a preview of many theories and techniques considered modern in institutions today, by the Civil War period moral treatment was virtually forgotten. In the 1890s philosopher William James would write, "Nowhere is massed together as much suffering as in the asylums. Nowhere is there so much sodden routine and fatalistic insensibility as in those who have to treat it . . . Public opinion is too glad to remain ignorant."

8

Phrenology and Mesmerism

Although the liberal mainstream of psychiatric thought during the first half of the nineteenth century favored the psychological approach, other theories about the causes of mental illness continued to be advanced and therapies based on these theories were often prescribed. Bloodletting was still common; physicians extracted as much as three to four quarts in some cases—frequently solving the problem by killing the patient. Blood transfusions, which had first been used in the eighteenth century and were thought to alter mood, had become fashionable. Reports tell of treatments which involved draining ten ounces of blood from the patient's arm and then transfusing part of this blood into a leg artery. As a further experiment, some patients were bled and then given transfusions of animal blood, with calves, dogs, and sheep the favored donors. When it was noted that some of the insane seemed to be cured of their mental confusion after a serious bout of fever, various attempts were made to infect the patient with fever-inducing elements—a form of therapy that would be tried again with better results in the twentieth century.

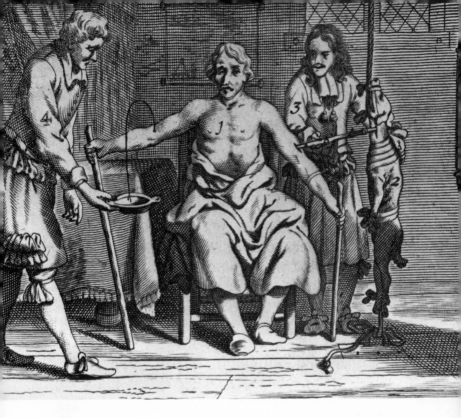

Man receiving a blood transfusion from a dog. National Library of Medicine, Bethesda, Md.

Despite the fact that there was little use of anesthesia until the second half of the century, operations were undertaken in the hope of curing insanity. Healthy teeth and sections of intestines were removed because of far-fetched theories. Masturbation was believed for centuries to lead to insanity, causing an untold amount of suffering, anxiety, and guilt in young and older men and women until recent decades, when the pioneering studies of sexuality by Dr. Alfred Kinsey found masturbation to be virtually universal and only its condemnation harmful. In the nineteenth century a particularly extreme view was taken of the situation. Operations to remove or desensitize sex organs were recommended procedures for stubborn cases and were carried out with shocking frequency. Scottish and English psychiatrists described "masturbatory insanity" as characterized by "extreme perversion of feeling and corresponding derangement of thought in its earlier stages, and later by failure of intelligence, nocturnal hallucinations, and suicidal and homicidal propensities." Faced with this dreadful threat, fathers locked sons into special contrivances at bedtime, which effectively prevented masturbation. One patented device for a male "chastity belt" was designed "to prevent involuntary nocturnal seminal emissions, to control waking thoughts, and to prevent self-abuse." Secured by a belt around the waist, it consisted of a metal plate with an opening through which the penis was to emerge. A sharp metal point attached to the upper part of the rim would jab sharply if the wearer had an erection. The inventor stated, "If the wearer be irresponsible from any cause, the appliance can be permanently secured to him."

Other methods for preventing and curing mental illness included a night's sleep in James Graham's "celestial bed" in his elaborate Aesculapian Temple. Graham, who called himself James Graham O.W.L. (Oh! Wonderful Love!), constructed a twelve-by-nine-foot bed which rested under blue lights on forty pillars of glass under a highly ornamental dome in a room wafted with incense and music. He alleged that his "Magnetico-Electrico" bed could cure all types of mental and physical illness and that children conceived after treatment were certain to enjoy a lifetime of good health.

Tub for therapeutic dousing. National Library of Medicine, Bethesda, Md.

More traditional therapists continued to support the theory that sudden shocks were curative, and patients were flung into bodies of water or startled by shots from cannons in an attempt to restore them to their senses. One physician urged that the patient, while seated in a tub, be drenched with two hundred pails of cold water, dropped on him from a height. An interest in "non-injurious torture" subjected the insane to pictures of lions' dens, playlets showing the dead rising from their graves, and visits to prisons and places of execution.

The nineteenth century also saw the development of the

phrenological movement. Phrenology—the study of the shape of the skull to determine intellectual capability and personality characteristics—was originated in Vienna by Franz Joseph Gall during the late eighteenth century. Gall was a physician who came to believe that mental faculties were inborn and did not change during a lifetime. He postulated that there were twenty-seven "organs" in the human brain and nineteen in those of animals—and that each organ was the site of certain mental and emotional characteristics that were established at birth. Bumps and depressions in the skull corresponded to these organs and became particularly protuberant over areas that were highly developed. Education and life experiences could not, according to Gall, alter these faculties.

Gall's theory was first inspired by his observation that a number of his most brilliant students had slightly bulging eyes. He deduced that the organ of memory was located directly behind the eyes, and that when strongly developed caused this characteristic protrusion. After observing many people and attempting to analyze their personalities, he palpated their skulls to locate areas of prominence. After a long series of studies made during visits to prisons and insane asylums, he felt confident that he was able to divide the contours of the skull, like a map, into sections which corresponded with personality traits. When he found several people with similar mental characteristics he would cast their heads in plaster and compare the conformations.

The medical establishment of Vienna would have nothing to do with such unorthodox theories and in 1802 Gall was forced to leave the city. He lectured widely in Europe and his most prominent disciple, John Caspar Spurzheim, advanced his theories on his own lecture circuit. When Spurzheim visited America in 1832 to lecture on phrenology, he was greeted as a prophet.

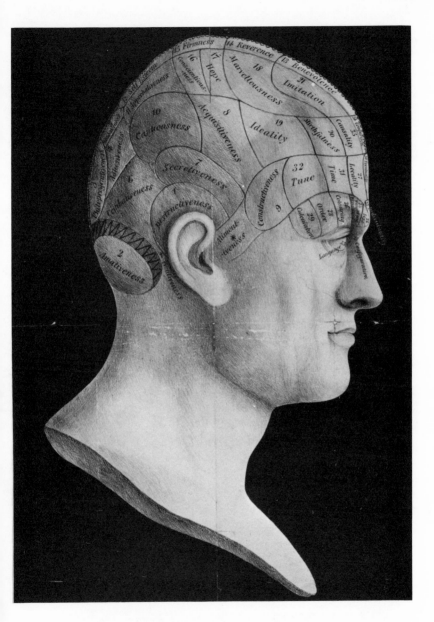

Phrenological head. Library of Congress.

Although "reading the bumps on a head" may sound absurd today, many American doctors of the nineteenth century adopted the techniques Gall had introduced and praised him highly. Pliny Earle, the much respected medical superintendent of the Northampton Asylum, went with his brother to have his head "read" and enthusiastically reported, "I doubt if any of my nearest relatives or most intimate friends could have given a more accurate synopsis of my character." Dr. William Awl (jestingly called "Dr. Cure-Awl"), visited a noted blind phrenologist who lost favor with the psychiatrist by pronouncing him underdeveloped in the area of intellectual strength. Educators found phrenology useful both for teaching purposes and for guiding children toward specific careers. Penologists diagnosed the instincts of criminals by studying their skulls. Celebrities of the time who found phrenology fascinating included Horace Mann, Walt Whitman, Edgar Allan Poe, and President James Garfield.

Both phrenological physicians and popular phrenologists concluded that a high degree of talent and intelligence caused overaction and overdevelopment of the brain, which could lead to brain inflammation and insanity. They recommended complete lack of intellectual exertion. Phrenological physicians tended to favor moral treatment, and psychiatrists practicing moral treatment in lunatic asylums often measured and palpated skulls of their patients with considerable interest and even made plaster casts to aid in diagnosis. Since the mind was thought to be divided into separate organs or compartments, articles in the *American Phrenological Journal* stated that insanity was not total but only partial, and treatment directed at reducing stress would permit the damaged brain surface of those affected parts to heal and would thus result in a cure. Examples of phrenological diagnoses were cited. A man was successfully treated with leeches and ice after it was found that he had been laughing uncontrollably since receiving a blow to the head over the organ of mirth. A woman developed a hysterical pregnancy due to overstimulation of the organ of love for children.

Later in the nineteenth century phrenology fell into disrepute. Skull reading as a form of fortune-telling became a sideshow feature at carnivals and serious people tended to debunk the entire matter. It is amusing to note that even when phrenology was at its height of popularity with intellectuals, there were skeptics in the ranks. John Quincy Adams said that he could not imagine how two phrenologists "could look each other in the face without bursting into laughter." The theory that definable areas of the brain control certain brain functions survived and later became a major concern of neurological research and the basis of psychosurgery.

Another Viennese physician, Anton Mesmer, was the originator of a theory which had considerable influence in the nineteenth century and which ultimately developed into the therapeutic tool known as hypnotism or hypnotic suggestion. Mesmer called his discovery "animal magnetism" but his followers dubbed it "mesmerism." In his book, *Memory and the Discovery of Animal Magnetism,* Mesmer discussed magnetism in the physical world. Man, said Mesmer, is also endowed with a particular magnetic fluid—an extra sense which, if liberated, can be used for healing. He believed that all disease resulted from disturbances of this magnetic fluid; and that the magnetizer, by releasing his own fluid, could effect a cure by causing the patient's own fluid to act on his unhealthy tissue. Mesmer experimented by transmitting his own magnetism to inanimate objects. He "magnetized" water, which patients then drank, and then he magnetized their clothing and their plates and even their bread.

Mesmer was a tall, handsome, romantic-looking man of humble origins. When he married a rich and very fashionable widow eleven years his senior, the elegant young doctor was welcomed into elite Viennese society. Apparently, he was a charmer—a witty and well-educated man who delighted women in particular with his good looks and fascinating conversation. He lived in a magnificent estate with a private theater in which Mozart operas were performed. Mesmer enjoyed his popularity and his luxurious life, but he experienced intense frustration in his career because of his compelling desire to have his theories of magnetism accepted and praised by men of science. He presented case reports of patients who had been cured by his use of animal magnetism, which were not regarded seriously by the people he hoped to impress. When he undertook to restore the vision of a beautiful young blind pianist it was rumored that his intention was sexual seduction.

At first Mesmer used actual magnets in his therapy, which he thought concentrated the magic magnetic fluid. Later he discarded the magnets as unnecessary when he came to believe that a simple gesture of his hands could convey and transmit magnetic force to his patient. Physicians were shocked by the idea that a medical man would attempt to cure by waving his hands like a faith healer. Like Joseph Gall, Mesmer was forced by conservative physicians of Vienna to depart for Paris, where Louis XVI had urged him to visit and conduct experiments in animal magnetism.

In Paris Mesmer was again acclaimed—by fashionable society. Wearing a lilac-colored cloak and carrying a magnetized wand, he would enter a dimly lit, mirrored room—thickly carpeted and filled with the sounds of music and the aroma of perfumes—in which a group of patients held hands in a circle around a basin of magnetized water. Mesmer would touch each participant with his wand and attempt to induce a trance state and then a "crisis"—sudden screams or convulsions indicating that magnetism was passing through the body. This was thought to be necessary for a cure. Since it was known that such a scene was expected to occur, mass suggestion seems to have

A Mesmeric seance. National Library of Medicine, Bethesda, Md.

been a vital factor. Mesmer's seances have been compared to revival meetings, in which the atmosphere becomes increasingly charged as people are seized with hypnotic frenzy.

Marie Antoinette offered Mesmer a considerable fee to continue his performances for Paris society, but Mesmer, who felt he had made a discovery of great importance to all mankind, suffered greatly from the fact that the medical recognition he sought still eluded him. A commission appointed to investigate animal magnetism—which included the famous Dr. Guillotin who was soon to lose his head on his own invention—found that no previously unknown magnetic fluid existed.

Interest in magnetism continued to spread despite the

Mesmerism. Woodcut after a drawing by Honoré Daumier. National Library of Medicine, Bethesda, Md.

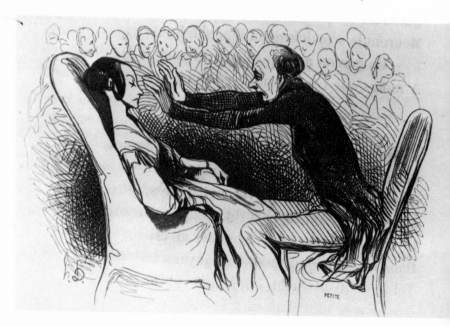

commission's report. In London James Graham placed magnetic baths around his celestial bed and assured clients that their influence would convey eternal health and sexual potency. In America a Yale Medical School graduate, Elisha Perkins, invented the Perkins Tractors, simple metal rods which were alleged to cure mental and physical ills by magnetic force.

Edgar Allan Poe wrote a tale called "The Facts in the Case of Mr. Valdemar," in which a magnetizer sustains a man's spirit in his dead body. In France, where faith in magnetism was greatest, the horror story was accepted as a factual account. One of Mesmer's enthusiastic French students, the Marquis de Puységur, placed a young peasant in a trance and told him, as he lay insensible, that when he awakened his illness would be gone. Apparently it worked. The technique of suggestion through hypnosis, which Puységur called "magnetic sleep," is still used by some therapists. In England "mesmerism" was employed to lessen pain in surgical procedures before anesthetic gases became accepted. One British doctor reported accomplishing 250 painless operations on Hindu convicts using mesmerism.

A skeptical Maine watchmaker named Phineas Parkhurst Quimby studied the new mesmerism and was told that since mesmeric action was electrical he should not use this force during a thunderstorm. When he disobeyed the rules and put a student in a trance outdoors during a summer torrent, he affirmed his doubt that the hypnotic force was electrical and became convinced that what he had demonstrated was simply "mind cure"—that the patient recovered because of faith in his therapist. Quimby had recognized a force once considered the property of shamans and priests and soon to be an acknowledged attribute of the physician. Healing by faith—in the healer or the method or both—has in one form or another served each generation.

In 1862 Quimby treated a woman named Mary Baker Glover Patterson who was handicapped by neurotic problems. She promptly recovered and queried him in detail about his "science of health." Her confidence in the relationship between faith and healing started her on a course of study and writing which led to the publication of her book *Science and Health* in 1875. After she married her third husband, co-worker Asa Gilbert Eddy, she became the founder of the Christian Science movement, a religion based on principles of divine healing. Christian Scientists believe that illness is an illusion which can be overcome by the mind. They refuse all treatment by physicians. Membership figures released in 1936—none have been published since, in accordance with Mrs. Eddy's prohibition against "numbering the people"—revealed that 250,000 Americans belonged to the Christian Science church, with additional members in most predominantly Protestant countries. It is believed that membership has declined since 1950, despite the absence of official statistics.

A new water cure known as hydropathy became known in this country during the nineteenth century, some years after it caught on in Europe. Hydropathists felt that physical and mental illnesses could be prevented—or, if too late, cured—by drinking and bathing in mineral waters. In the 1840s a number of hydropathic establishments sprang up on the east coast where patients bathed and showered in warm water and cold water, lay under wet packs, suffered injections of water into their bodies, and relaxed—naturally—in steam baths. The theory behind this treatment was that disease, defined as inflammation, is relieved when the application of water draws blood from the inflamed area. Also, with such large intakes of water there was a corresponding increase in output of urine. It was thought that the dangerous morbid matter causing disease would be passed from the body in this fashion. Hydropathy was widely recommended for the insane and many people brought mentally deranged relatives to the new spas.

In the asylums mild drugs were used to render patients more subdued and ready to accept moral therapy. Old remedies—purges and emetics—continued. A British medical book recommends "the relaxing system for a fortnight or three weeks but not less than a fortnight; then to administer two or three smart vomits in as many days" followed by "smart purges." After that, sudden shocks, by means of plunges into cold water and the violent motion of the swing, are recommended. If this fails the writer suggests that the patient be given enough strong drink to render him intoxicated—and that the course of therapy be repeated. Other physicians insisted that all activities which bring blood to the head, such as walking in hot weather, alcoholic drinks, swimming, stooping, riding horseback, be avoided. Most agreed that the head should be kept shaved—and, therefore, cool. Hellebore, that favorite remedy of the Greeks, was still in good stead with many nineteenth-century practitioners.

As the century progressed, physical restraints, which had never entirely disappeared, were used more and more frequently. The straitjacket—a garment with long sleeves which extend beyond the hands, enabling the doctor to secure the patient's arms behind his back or against his chest—was thought by many to have actual therapeutic benefits, much like those of Benjamin Rush's tranquilizing chair. Advocates claimed that it induced a reflective frame of mind and assisted mental relaxation as well as physical slow-down. The "muff," in which the patient's hands were encased and joined in mufflike gloves, prevented him

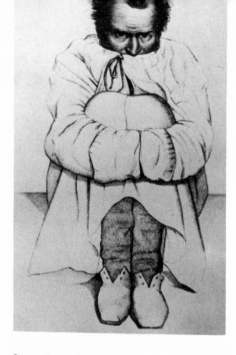

The muff.
American
Psychiatric
Association
Archives.

from harming himself or others, and also from masturbating.

By the last quarter of the nineteenth century developments which were to lead to the beginning of the modern era of "dynamic psychiatry" were under way. A new age was at hand. Advances in neurology after the Civil War first led to physical treatments for neurological ailments and injuries and soon became the basis of attacks on psychological ills with symptoms that imitated physical diseases. Old beliefs, however, persisted, and leading surgeons removed ovaries from hundreds of thousands of women who exhibited signs of hysteria. Jean Martin Charcot, head of the Salpêtrière and the leading neurologist of the period, approved of such surgery, but he also began studies of the use of hypnosis on severely hysterical patients confined to the vast old institution. These experiments were to be of the greatest possible interest to a young physician from Vienna named Sigmund Freud.

9
Psychoanalysis:
The Modern Era

Before the 1890s, the only people considered mentally ill were the "madmen" or "lunatics"—people who suffered from the totally disabling forms of illness we now call psychoses. It was at the end of the nineteenth century that neurologists and then psychiatrists began studying and treating the less handicapped neurotics as well as the psychotics. The theory and method of psychoanalysis, originated by Sigmund Freud, a Viennese neurologist, was directly inspired by contemporary interest in treating the type of neurosis known as hysteria. It is important to realize that Freud's ideas formed a genuine revolution in thought —a breakthrough from ignorance to an understanding of the nature of man's psychological makeup. Like Copernicus, Newton, or Darwin, he made scientific discoveries that totally changed people's basic concepts about themselves and their world. Many of the theories he postulated in the late nineteenth and early twentieth centuries shocked and outraged his fellow scientists, but they have now become such an accepted part of the average lay person's thinking that today they are scarcely attributed to Freud at all but are thought of instead as old undisputed truths.

The specific terms and descriptions by which one form

of psychiatric illness is differentiated from another have been developed since the 1890s, replacing earlier attempts at classification. It is essential to understand these broad distinctions between forms of illness before talking about twentieth-century approaches to therapy.

The major mental illnesses, the psychoses, are—unlike the neuroses—characterized by a loss of the sense of reality with severe disturbance of both thought and emotion. The patient is often unable to distinguish between the subjective world of his mental processes and the objective world outside his own person. Psychosis is a violent affliction involving personality disintegration which, in its most severe form, leaves the victim totally unable to deal with himself or his surroundings.

Schizophrenia is the most common psychosis, although the term is used to cover a number of different forms of the disease. The acute schizophrenic is disordered in thought and in expression. His behavior often seems strange and meaningless. He may experience hallucinations in which he sees visions and hears voices, and he may attempt to kill or mutilate himself in response to commands from invisible sources. He may believe he has been transformed into another person—even a deity—or he may feel damned, intensely fearful of impending punishment or catastrophe. He may be certain that others are persecuting him, that strangers wish him harm and are conspiring against him. He may be violently excited, destructive, aggressive, or he may be mute and motionless, like someone in a trance. Schizophrenia is most likely to occur for the first time in young adulthood, and some forms, such as autism, manifest themselves in infancy and early childhood.

Depressive and manic-depressive psychosis involve less disorganization of the personality than full-blown schizophrenia, although thought and emotion can be wildly out of control. The patient has long and intense periods of depression, during which he feels totally without hope, evil, worthless; overwhelmed by gloom and despair, guilt and remorse. Suicidal thoughts may become obsessive. Depression or excitement ("mania") may occur alone or as one stage of a cyclical disease known as manic-depressive psychosis, in which the sick person alternates between periods of deep despondency and periods of great elation. The manic person, unlike the schizophrenic or the depressive patient, feels euphoric, filled with energy, stimulated by ideas and plans of great importance. He may spend all his money phoning people around the world, investing in irrational business schemes or in grandiose programs of his own devising designed to alter global problems, end wars, eliminate poverty. Between periods of explosive elation and other periods of massive depression, the patient may enjoy months or years of normal mood, thought, and behavior.

The psychoses are now thought to have their origin in both genetic factors and psychological stresses. Other forms of psychosis marked by mental confusion, depression, and aggressiveness can be brought on by specific physical illnesses that ultimately affect brain function, such as syphilis, brain tumor, hardening of the arteries in elderly people, or by alcoholism or intoxication by poisons.

Neuroses are typified by conflicts within the personality that are thought—since Freud first described them psychoanalytically—to stem from early childhood experiences. The neuroses are generally considered to be entirely psychological in origin, although scientists feel that there must be an inherited vulnerability to account for the fact that some people suffer mental illness following traumatic childhoods and others do not. We use the term "neurotic" freely in ordinary conversation to describe a person who is fussy, temperamental, self-preoccupied, or timid. We view neurosis correctly as something extra and unnecessary, an exaggeration of troubling emotions familiar to us all—a mental burden a person may carry about throughout life which bears little relationship to the unavoidable external problems of everyday existence.

The fact is that most of us have some personality traits that limit our freedom—our ability to act in ways we might like. We have anxieties and we have phobias: feelings of inferiority, uneasiness about new situations, unreasoning fears of open places, closed-in places, heights, cats, mice, even foods. We may have repetitive thoughts that echo in our heads and distract us from concentrating on what we are doing. We may perform such silly rituals as arranging our possessions in a certain set order or going back four times to be sure we have not left a door unlocked before leaving the house. We fear death, illness, loss of another person's love, and such fears can become very painful. To the severe neurotic these forms of thought and behavior can be so compelling that they interfere with the ability to feel healthy, to form and enjoy personal relationships, to keep a job, to make a successful sexual adjustment, to eat, to sleep. Neurosis can make life total misery regardless of the fact that the sufferer may seem to others to be healthy, handsome, and highly privileged. Unlike the psychotic, the neurotic is aware of the fact that it is unreasonable to be so fearful or so depressed. This knowledge may add to his despair.

"Neurotic" is a broad term covering a variety of sufferers. Obsessive-compulsives feel an unreasonable need to repeat certain rituals. Most obsessive behavior is viewed as an attempt to keep repressed thoughts or emotions in the unconscious area of the mind. Excessive hand-washing may result from guilt, as Shakespeare knew when he had Lady Macbeth try repeatedly to scrub invisible blood from her hands. Even a rigid routine of arranging objects in a room or on a desk may be a form of obsessive-compulsive behavior. Compulsive cleanliness is a common symptom. Most of us have some fear of germs and a distaste for dirt, but there are people whose anxiety about uncleanliness is so severe that they cannot carry money, eat in a public place, open a door without putting on gloves. Some totally incapacitated victims cannot get out of bed for fear of contacting dirt on the floor.

Phobias are unreasonable fears, such as the fear of heights when there is no danger involved, or of open places, enclosed places, or harmless insects or animals. A severe phobia causing dizziness, nausea, and panic is viewed by psychiatrists as an attempt to turn an interior problem outward. A socially disapproved emotion—such as intense fear or hatred of a parent—can be repressed and may emerge many years later in the more acceptable form of a phobia. But a phobia can turn into a severe handicap. A person who is so alarmed by heights or by elevators that he cannot take a job or live in an apartment above the ground floor is in serious trouble.

Depression, of the neurotic rather than the psychotic variety, is, like many neuroses, exaggeration of a common emotion. It is healthy to feel dejected after a disappointment or a loss, to sometimes have the "blues"—to feel lonely, sad, inadequate in some area of life. The person with a more severe neurotic depression feels despondent for long periods of time or for no apparent reason. He may feel unjustifiably unloved and worthless. He may be unable to eat and may have other bodily symptoms such as constant fatigue, insomnia, headaches, constipation. His despair may become so severe as to make him feel that suicide is the only solution.

Anxiety reaction is again a more disabling form of the familiar sense of apprehension, the feeling that something very unfortunate or unpleasant may happen. A mother experiences anxiety when her children seem exposed to the risk of contagious illness. A student may feel very nervous and anxious about facing the first day at a new school. The neurotic parent, however, may feel an obsessive dread that the child will develop or has developed some rare or fatal disease. A neurotic young person may actually be unable to enter the new school and may arrive at the door and then flee day after day.

Conversion reaction, which was formerly called hysteria, is a neurosis in which an unacceptable emotion finds an outlet in a severe physical symptom. The Greeks attributed hysteria to dislocation of the uterus, but it is now viewed as a psychological disease which can occur in men as well as in women. Hysterical symptoms mimic symptoms of physical disease: blindness, deafness, paralysis of a limb, loss of sensation over some part of the body. Although the neurosis stems from earlier life, a current crisis can bring on a severe hysterical reaction. Soldiers have suddenly become totally paralyzed at the battlefront. An auto accident which causes no actual injury may be the frightening event which leaves the victim with medically unexplainable pain or loss of function.

Other mental disorders besides psychoses and neuroses include mental retardation, psychosomatic disorders in which emotional factors may cause an actual physical ailment, and a long list of so-called personality disorders. Unlike the neuroses, which are all characterized by anxiety, the personality disorders are most often lifelong patterns of behavior which seem inappropriate but do not appear to cause the patient concern or a desire to change. People with personality disorders may be unable to express normal aggressive feelings, seem unaffected by disturbing experiences, seem unable to be emotionally close or competitive with others. They may be irresponsible and constantly in conflict with social values, but have no ability to learn from these unpleasant experiences or to feel guilt. Other disorders include uncontrollable outbursts of rage and such sexual deviations as sadism, masochism, fetishism, exhibitionism, transvestism. The personality disorders and, most successfully, the neuroses or "psychoneuroses" are now being treated by a great number of psychotherapies, all of which derive in some fashion from Sigmund Freud's theories about the conflict between conscious and unconscious levels of desire.

Interest in the unconscious did not originate with Freud. Earlier speculations on the subject had been voiced during the nineteenth century, usually by philosophers and poets. Mesmer and his followers, although they used a different vocabulary to describe their ideas, were trying to contact the unconscious through hypnotism.

The scientific study of the therapeutic use of hypnosis began with the investigations of the famous neurologist Jean Martin Charcot in the 1870s. Charcot had become the first professor of nervous diseases at the Salpêtrière, the vast institution for women in Paris where Pinel had unchained patients a century earlier. At this time psychotic patients confined to mental hospitals were treated by psychiatrists, but people with hysterical symptoms were generally directed to the practitioners of the new medical specialty, neurology. The neurologist would examine the paralyzed limb or area of numbness and try to establish the presence of a physical disorder through his knowledge of the distribution of motor and sensory nerves.

Transferring his interest from the physical to the psychological aspects of his specialty, Charcot began to study severe hysterics. He found that he could use hypnotism to induce the paralyses and areas of numbness that mark the hysterical reaction, and he became convinced that there was a psychological factor in their origin. Soon afterward he demonstrated that hysterical symptoms could be cured by hypnotic suggestion. A patient would be put into a trance and told that when he awakened his problem would be gone. Charcot believed that only hysterics could be hypnotized.

In the city of Nancy, Hippolyte Bernheim, another brilliant neurologist, disputed Charcot's claim that only hysterics could be hypnotized—and proved that he was right. In Bernheim's view almost anyone could be hypnotized and would then be susceptible to curative suggestions.

Sigmund Freud was born in 1856 in Freiberg, Moravia, then part of Austria and now in Czechoslovakia. The son of a poor Jewish family—his father was a country wool merchant—he displayed from an early age scientific curiosity, intellectual superiority, and a driving desire to excel. As a medical student he was particularly interested in physiology, but after receiving his degree he turned his attention to neurology and went to Paris to study under Charcot.

When Freud returned to Vienna he was imbued with Charcot's faith in the value of hypnosis in treating hysteria, and he continued his work under the added influence of a prominent Austrian physician, Josef Breuer. They found that patients under hypnosis lost their inhibitions about discussing their problems, and that this catharsis or release of formerly blocked emotions seemed to bring about a cure for hysterical symptoms. Josef Breuer had used hypnosis in this way to treat a patient who would become famous in the annals of psychiatry under the pseudonym of "Anna O."

Anna O. was a highly intelligent and attractive twenty-one-year-old woman who presented a variety of hysterical symptoms. Her right arm and leg were paralyzed; her eyesight had suddenly become severely impaired; she suffered from nausea, from confusion, from disturbing personality changes. Although she seemed to be afflicted by a severe physical illness she had no evidence of disease or injury. Breuer placed the patient in a state of hypnosis in which she freely discussed her deepest emotions. Anna O. had spent considerable time nursing her ailing father and had become ill after his death. It became apparent as she talked that repressed feelings she had toward her father and the constraints of having to care for him were related to her symptoms. As she talked about herself under hypnosis the symptoms disappeared. The patient herself referred to her treatment as "the talking cure"—a description still often used by lay people today for psychotherapy in general. Neurologists of the period called it "the cathartic method."

Sigmund Freud also studied the case of Anna O. and later wrote about it with Breuer. When Breuer's wife became jealous of the amount of time he was spending with his absorbing patient, he concluded treatment, telling Anna O. that she was now well and no longer needed his attention. That evening Breuer was summoned to her bedside. The greatly agitated former patient was in the throes of a hysterical childbirth. She had become convinced that she was pregnant and that the father of her child was her psychiatrist, Josef Breuer. Breuer calmed her by the use of hypnosis and then ran from the house in alarm. The eminent doctor decided he had had enough of the problems of hysterics, but Freud discovered a phenomenon which he was to call "transference"—the way in which patients "transfer" to the psychoanalyst emotions they previously felt toward other important people in their lives. The transference is an irrational resurrection of old unresolved emotions, often those of the child for the parent, and Anna O's amorous fantasies about her doctor surfaced in her mock pregnancy. It is interesting to note that, although she was intermittently bothered with symptoms all her life, Anna O. became the first social worker in Germany, developed an intense and productive interest in women's emancipation, did significant work with children, and founded a number of schools at which students were trained to go into social work.

The development of Freud's theories of conflict, of the significance of dreams, of transference in the analytic relationship developed over a period of years as he attempted to treat patients suffering from a variety of severe neurotic disabilities. Freud postulated that neuroses develop from the early childhood conflict between the mainstream of conscious thinking and the stream of unacceptable desires which are suppressed in the unconscious. As the child grows and develops, all the ideas and wants that provoke guilt—most of which Freud thought were sexual—are pushed into the unconscious part of the psyche or mind and forgotten. Although this process was viewed as an essential part of normal development, Freud theorized that these repressions could emerge in later life in the form of neurotic conflicts.

The theory and the method of psychoanalysis developed side by side, inextricably intertwined. Freud felt that patients must be helped to recall painful and unresolved conflicts of early life. He soon observed, however, that they resisted recalling painful experiences which they had successfully repressed. In 1896 he wrote describing these "defensive" operations. He also described his method of breaking through these defenses and called it "psychoanalysis." He realized that this resistance was the same force that initially pushed painful emotional experiences into the unconscious. He wrote that the goal of treatment was "making conscious what is unconscious, lifting repression, filling gaps in the memory." The patient could then examine emotions he had repressed for so long, reevaluate childish motives, gain self-knowledge, and ultimately achieve a cure.

To encourage this process the method of treatment was standardized. Freud had begun his work with all types of neurotics using techniques of hypnosis which he had learned from Charcot and Breuer, but soon he discovered a new technique. Rather than putting the patient into a trance, he helped him explore painful past emotional experiences by teaching him "free association." He urged the patient to lie in a relaxed position on a couch and to begin to talk, expressing every thought that entered his head no matter how shameful or trivial or nonsensical it seemed. The analyst was to sit out of sight behind the patient rather than facing him, to foster the patient's ability to free associate. When we are talking to someone face-to-face we watch for signs of how our ideas are being received and we expect verbal responses. In the psychoanalytic situation, it is essential to be able to speak without inhibition, without waiting for a response.

Sigmund Freud.
Drawing by David Levine.
Reprinted with permission
from The New York
Review of Books.
Copyright © *1967*
NYRev Inc.

Freud made a number of discoveries as he listened to the recollections of his patients and as he engaged in an extended self-analysis. He was struck over and over by the fact that staid middle-class Viennese men and women were describing lurid childhood sexual experiences. Had these proper children from privileged homes actually been raped by their fathers, seduced by their sisters, lured to bed by their mothers? Freud doubted it. He postulated that the unconscious does not distinguish between fact and fantasy

—that these tales of seduction in early life were fantasies and that these fantasies derived from wishes.

The next twenty years were spent in investigating the source of these unacceptable fantasies. Freud studied dreams in the first truly scientific attempt to understand the fantasies or wishes which occur when, in the sleeping state, we are relieved of the inhibiting restrictions we apply to daytime thoughts. The ancient practice of dream analysis had always been related to the foretelling of the future. The Freudian view of dreams is that they relate to the past. In sleep we partially escape the censor in our brain which tells us that improper desires should be cast aside. Because some defenses against unacceptable desires still persist in sleep, dreams are often symbolic. The young child who dreams that wild animals are chasing him, for example, may fear that his strong and powerful father is going to kill him in retribution for his own desire to do away with his father. Helping the patient interpret his dreams became an important aspect of psychoanalysis.

Just as a dream is a compromise between an unacceptable wish and the personality's defenses against it, so, said Freud, is a symptom. Anna O.'s paralyzed arm represented a compromise between her dutiful attention to her dying father and her wish to strike him dead so she could go off to a dance with other young people. In the psychoanalytic process, in which the person purges himself of these handicapping conflicts by bringing them to awareness, transference must take place and later reach resolution. Through the transference the patient "relives" the early conflicts with parents. The analyst, however, does not respond with punishment or disapproval. Hidden and unacceptable feelings can be reenacted without fear of retribution. The transference does not occur with patients suffering from psychoses, since their disorder makes them incapable of forming deep personal bonds, and for that reason psychoanalysis has remained a technique best suited to the treatment of neuroses.

Freud used the term "Oedipus complex" to express what he conceived to be the young child's sexual desire for the parent of the opposite sex—and his subsequent fantasy of somehow getting rid of the parent of the same sex whom he wishes to replace. This conflict is rapidly suppressed and pushed into the child's unconscious, but it can continue to influence development and adult behavior. Usually the resolution of the Oedipal conflict occurs at the end of early childhood—at about the age for entering school—and the child then makes a massive identification with the moral values of both his parents. He steps out into the world with less interest in his parents and a greater desire to be with other children. He has a strong sense of himself as a person separate from his mother and father.

Many severe neuroses result from failure to resolve the Oedipal conflict at the appropriate stage of development. A woman who was afraid to make an emotional commitment to any man discovered in analysis that the source of her problem was her sense of total abandonment when her father left home for the army when she was five, and experiencing her period of greatest emotional attachment to him. This intense disappointment, pushed into her unconscious, had ever after reflected itself in an inability to form strong bonds to members of the opposite sex. A defense mechanism which worked well for her in early life had become a serious impediment to fulfillment as an adult.

Freud's theories of human development expanded

throughout his long, extraordinarily productive life. Although he had hosts of adoring students and disciples, it was many years before his concepts were widely acknowledged. When he read papers before medical societies about unconscious sexual conflicts in young children, people were shocked and repelled. Although his landmark book, *The Interpretation of Dreams*, was published in 1900, it was not until 1920 that he began to be accepted in European psychiatric circles.

Acceptance came earlier in America than in Europe. In 1909 the fifty-three-year-old Freud was given an honorary degree at Clark University in Worcester, Massachusetts, the only honorary degree he was ever to receive. The American psychiatrists and psychologists greeted him with great acclaim. "In Europe I felt as though I were despised," he wrote later, "but over there I found myself received by the foremost men as an equal." The new psychoanalytic theories and methods rapidly replaced other contemporary approaches in this country.

Freud's two most gifted pupils, Alfred Adler and Carl Gustav Jung, joined him in 1906, and although both were to defect in less than ten years to develop their own systems, Freud's large group of enthusiastic students and co-workers included such well-known people as Otto Rank, Hanns Sachs, Ernest Jones, Abraham Brill, and Sandor Ferenczi. His youngest daughter Anna became a brilliant psychoanalyst and a leader in developmental studies of children. Among other famous female psychoanalysts who expanded on or deviated from Freudian theory were Karen Horney, who came to believe that neuroses stemmed from conflict between human beings rather than between the social environment and the instincts; Melanie Klein, who did important work with children; and Helen

Deutsch, a pioneer in female psychology. Alfred Adler founded the child guidance movement. C. G. Jung formulated his own method of "analytical psychology" and his own theories about the libido and the unconscious and contributed to our understanding of symbolism with his mystical focus on racial and collective memories.

Freud was a man of far-ranging intellectual interests and abilities. His passionate hobby was archeology and he collected Greek and Egyptian antiquities, followed the news of excavations, retained a lifelong interest in the classical literature, in poetry, sculpture, architecture, and painting. He wrote extensively and was the master of a fine literary style. He was very fond of children, had a happy marriage, and was the father of three boys and three girls.

In the early 1930s Freud's books were burned by the Nazis, but there were grand celebrations in a number of countries on his eightieth birthday in 1936. He was urged by friends and co-workers to leave Austria as the Nazi threat grew but he refused to leave Vienna, where he had lived since the age of four, until the Nazis actually invaded in March 1938. His four surviving sisters remained in Vienna and died in Nazi concentration camps. Freud himself died of cancer in London on September 23, 1939, at the age of eighty-three.

10
Electroshock,
Psychopharmacology,
Psychosurgery

Greek physicians of the fifth century B.C. believed that mental illness was caused by physical imbalance and should be treated with such physical remedies as bleeding and purging and medication—and their advice was followed for almost two and a half millennia. Down through the centuries any number of additional therapies have been proposed, invented, and recommended by optimistic and imaginative physicians. A sixteenth-century medical text offered this advice: "A roasted mous eaten doth heale Franticke persons." Most of the odd and time-honored organic treatments designed to cure the mentally ill now seem harmful, cruel, or simply ineffective.

Today the "disturbed" wards of mental hospitals are quiet places because of highly successful physical approaches conceived only decades ago. Restraining harnesses and packs of cold wet sheets now seem as obsolete as chains and barred cribs. The most seriously ill patients—those suffering from complete loss of a sense of reality and responsive to no psychological treatment—have been reached through drug therapies, shock therapy, or psychosurgery, and restored to unhoped-for levels of function.

The Greek theory that mental illness might have a physical explanation and be successfully treated by physical means was given new credence with the discovery of the organic cause of, and a successful treatment for, general paresis. This condition had been described in the nineteenth century by such names as "paralytic insanity" and attributed to a softening or chronic inflammation of the brain. It was theorized that men were more commonly afflicted than women because they were more subject to head injuries and more likely to be alcoholic. Soldiers were noted to show a high incidence of the disease, and this fact was attributed to privations associated with battle, which were thought to make one more susceptible to inflammation. It was treated by current therapies for other forms of mental illness—bleeding, laxatives, clysters, plasters, and shaving of the head.

It was not until 1904 that Emil Kraepelin wrote, "Syphilitic infection is an essential for the later appearance of paresis." In 1912 specific tests for syphilitic conditions were performed by tapping cerebrospinal fluid of paretics through the technique of lumbar puncture, in which a needle was inserted into the spinal canal between the vertebrae of the lower back. In 1917 Wagner von Jauregg experimented by innoculating nine victims of paresis with malaria parasite. Studies were continued at St. Elizabeth's Hospital in Washington, D.C., and at the New York Psychiatric Institute in the 1920s, and remissions were noted in 30 percent of cases. Although belief in the fact that high fever could cure mental illness dates to ancient Greece and Rome, the specific success in these well-controlled experiments was a landmark in psychiatric history. In 1927 the significance of von Jauregg's work was recognized when he was awarded the Nobel Prize.

Researchers avidly sought organic causes and cures

for other types of mental illness in the genes, in infections, in metabolic or nutritional diseases. Pellagra, which also caused mental symptoms, was found to be a nutritional disorder due to vitamin B deficiency and curable by correct diet. Geneticists found that PKU—phenylketonuria, a disease which is accompanied by severe mental retardation—was caused by inborn metabolic error.

In the 1920s an increased interest in finding biological explanations for mental illness led to attempts to predict the likelihood of various kinds of psychoses on the basis of bodily type. Ernst Kretschmer in Germany and W. H. Sheldon in the United States classified people by broad physical type: the endomorph (rotund, flabby), the mesomorph (muscular, athletic), and the ectomorph (thin). Mesomorphs were considered the least likely to develop mental illness. Ectomorphs were thought more prone to schizophrenia than people of other body types, and endomorphs were considered more likely to become manic-depressive. Other studies were undertaken to demonstrate the occurrence of mental illness in children or siblings of schizophrenics in an attempt to demonstrate hereditary influence.

The search for physical explanations for mental illness and the development of organic therapies have paralleled interest in and research on purely psychological theories and approaches. But the development of organic treatments, unlike that of the psychotherapies, has often proceeded simply on the basis of success without substantiating explanations or theories as to *why* the desired result takes place. Major questions still remain unanswered. Today three therapies—electroconvulsive (electroshock) therapy, psychosurgery, and psychopharmacology (drug treatment) —are the major organic weapons against mental illness. Each was greeted initially as a virtual cure-all for the most difficult to treat psychoses. Today all are used selectively. Drug therapies, because they are relatively safe and easily administered, have now virtually replaced psychosurgery and have considerably reduced the use of electroconvulsive therapy. Psychosurgery has become the most controversial of the organic therapies, opening new areas of moral—not simply medical—debate. All three therapies have been used in conjunction with psychiatric counseling in a combined organic-psychiatric approach.

Electroconvulsive Therapy

Electroconvulsive therapy—better known by the less accurate term "electroshock"—was first tried in the 1930s and became the enthusiastically accepted treatment of choice for schizophrenia, mania, and depression in the 1940s and 1950s. Like most modern therapies it had, at least in theory, a number of precedents in the history of the treatment of the mentally ill. The idea of administering a physical shock to the nervous system to restore rationality was the basis for dousings with ice cold water and agonizing rotations on mechanical swings in the eighteenth and nineteenth centuries. Jolting the body with electric current was an even older idea. Galen had used shocks from electric fish to treat both physical and mental illnesses. Benjamin Franklin, who was not at all reluctant to play physician, treated a number of different diseases with the use of the Leyden jar, a glass jar coated inside and out with conductive metal foil and fitted with a conducting rod to transmit the charge. In 1755 one Richard Lovett used the first electric condenser to treat mental disease with electric currents. Apparently he and Franklin were not the only dabblers in the art because a book of the period cautions would-be electric-shock therapists who do not have medi-

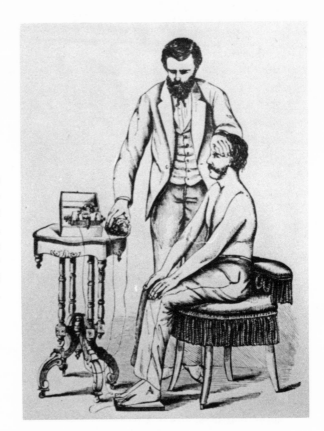

Faradization in the nineteenth century. American Psychiatric Association Archives.

cal background, "It is not sufficient to know how to turn the handle of an electric machine."

In the nineteenth century a range of physical and mental problems were assaulted with electricity. As early as 1801 an experimenter claims to have cured hysterical paralysis and stupor by using direct continuous current from a machine of his invention. By mid-century, faradic current was thought to be stimulating, galvanic current calming, and both were tried on patients suffering from insomnia, melancholy, headaches, impotence, idiocy, constipation, menstrual problems, neuralgia, and muscle weakness.

Although most investigators were European, American doctors were also curious about the potential therapeutic uses of electric current. During the last half of the nineteenth century, it was felt that gentle applications, given in daily sessions which might go on for as long as a month, were more beneficial than fewer stronger exposures. Convulsive reactions were observed but were considered a highly undesirable effect and obvious proof of excessive current.

More carefully focused forms of investigation were resumed in the 1930s based on the observation that seriously ill mental patients seemed to be restored to reason after having a spontaneous convulsion as the result of high fever or some other physical distress. Researchers also observed that epilepsy and schizophrenia never seemed to occur in the same patient. It became apparent that the occurrence of a seizure, for whatever reason, could alleviate the symptoms of the major mental illnesses.

The first attempts to produce convulsions were made with chemical rather than electrical stimuli. In 1935 intravenous injections of camphor in oil were tried, but difficulty in estimating whether or not the patient would have a convulsion, and if so when it would occur, made this an unsatisfactory method. It was discovered that a synthetic camphor solution known as Metrazol would produce a convulsion within thirty seconds in most patients. Although Metrazol treatment is still in very limited use, it was virtually superseded by the introduction of electroconvulsive treatment (ECT) by two Italian psychiatrists, Ugo Cerletti and L. Bini, who had experimented on hogs at a Roman slaughterhouse to determine safe electrical dosages.

Today's technique, which varies only in minor details from one center to another, involves the application of about 400 milliamperes of alternating current through electrodes attached to the temples with a conductive jelly of the type used when a doctor makes electrocardiogram tracings of heart activity. The current is sent through the brain at about 100 volts, producing a convulsion which lasts less than a minute (as comparison with what we know to be a lethal dose; electric chairs use 7-ampere current at about 50,000 volts).

In the early years of ECT severe and highly distressing complications in the form of fractured bones and teeth occurred during convulsions. Today drugs which actually cause temporary paralysis of the muscles are given before treatment and they have effectively eliminated the problem. The standard procedure involves routine injection of these strong relaxants, preceded by a light anesthesia to assure that the patient will be spared as much anxiety as possible. Mouth gags are used to prevent injury to the teeth or tongue during convulsion since jaw muscles continue to clamp tightly despite strong medication.

Electroconvulsive treatment is given in series of varying durations depending on the illness and its severity. A course of as many as eleven to fourteen treatments over a four- to five-week span is not rare. Although most people respond with an immediate brief convulsion, it is often observed that women seem to require a stronger current than men, and older people more than younger. The patient is unconscious during his convulsion. After electroconvulsive treatment patients regain consciousness within a few minutes but may remain in a confused mental state for considerably longer. When treatment is given to someone who is not hospitalized, the patient is usually able to be taken home in about an hour. He has no memory of the treatment afterward and may later have amnesia for the entire series. Many people also find that they have blank spaces in their recollection of events during a period of some weeks after treatment is concluded. Although some patients feel that their memory has been permanently impaired by ECT, many doctors state that there is no medical evidence that this is actually true.

No one knows at this time *how* ECT works to alleviate symptoms of severe mental illness but results are usually rapid and dramatic. Although it was originally conceived as a treatment for schizophrenia, the greatest success has been in the treatment of depression, and it is mainly for this condition that it is used today. Before the advent of the antipsychotic drugs it was considered the most effective therapy for psychosis, but it is still—while in much more limited use—a major weapon against disabling illness. ECT has been used to relieve severe psychotic depressions of both recent and long-term variety and, by some psychiatrists, for the less incapacitating neurotic depressions.

In 1972 presidential candidate George McGovern chose as his vice-presidential running mate Senator Thomas Eagleton. The fact that Eagleton had been treated by ECT for depression received sensational publicity and Eagleton withdrew his acceptance of the nomination. Many Americans were horrified to imagine that a man with a past psychiatric illness might have achieved such high office and were astounded at reports that serious cases of depression currently afflict 5 and 10 million Americans, according to National Institute of Mental Health figures. Millions more suffer milder forms of depression. Many never seek treatment, and of those who do, therapy will vary according to the preferences of the psychiatrist consulted. The fact that one depressed patient is treated with psychotherapy and another with shock is often a reflection of the persuasion of the treating psychiatrist rather than of the relative gravity of the condition.

It is important to realize that ECT treats symptoms and not basic causes of disease. Often ECT is used for rapid relief of symptoms—particularly in patients considered suicidal—and is then followed up by the use of antidepressant drugs and some form of psychotherapy as well. When convulsive therapy is used to treat schizophrenia, rapid relapses have proven a danger unless treatment is continued.

An earlier form of therapy which relies on drugs rather than on electricity to induce unconsciousness is now used to only a minimal degree. Known as insulin coma treatment, it was developed after physicians noted that psychotic diabetic patients who went into coma due to insulin dosage problems often showed greatly improved mental function afterwards. In addition, in the 1920s psychotic patients who were often given small dosages of insulin to stimulate appetite showed evidence of improvement in their emotional condition. In 1933 Manfred Sakel of Berlin experimented in treating schizophrenics by inducing insulin shock. This is easily accomplished by injecting insulin, which drops the level of sugar in the blood and the amount of oxygen as well. The brain is highly sensitive to oxygen deprivation, and at a certain level the patient goes into a coma. Although such an occurrence can be life-threatening, under careful medical supervision the technique has been used successfully in the treatment of severe mental illness. Insulin shock, unlike electric shock, is considered highly dangerous to many people, and a number of well-trained attendants are required for each treatment.

Today, although some authorities feel it provides better results in selected cases, insulin shock has been virtually abandoned and replaced by ECT, which is very much easier to administer and less likely to produce any unfavorable side effects. Although ECT does not prevent relapse of illness, the rapidity with which it alters mood has kept it in favor as a valuable treatment for depression and some other forms of mental illness, particularly when combined with further physical and psychiatric therapy.

Psychopharmacology

The use of drugs to alleviate mental illness or alter mood dates back to earliest times when concoctions of plants and herbs thought to have medicinal properties were prepared by medicine men, lay healers, and physicians. In some Mediterranean countries opium and alcohol were used for their sedative effect at least as early as 1000 B.C. Hashish, brought back to France from Egypt by Napoleonic soldiers and explorers, was suggested as a treatment for depression in 1845. The search for an effective tranquilizer for people suffering from agitated forms of mental illness led to widespread use of opium in mental institutions in the mid-nineteenth century but increasing awareness of the addictive qualities of the drug brought about its abandonment several decades later. Other drugs used in the nineteenth and twentieth centuries as sedatives or to relieve anxiety and depression include tartrate of antimony, ipecac, digitalis, calomel, belladonna, quinine, chloral, bromides, paraldehyde, and the barbiturates, which were introduced in 1903. Freud experimented enthusiastically with cocaine as a mood elevator until he became convinced that some people formed addictions to the drug.

As each new medication was found to be of some benefit to mental patients it was greeted with immense optimism. All in turn, however, were found to have certain grave limitations and were later prescribed infrequently if at all, or in a more limited fashion for carefully specified conditions.

The modern age of psychopharmacology—which has

resulted in a wide span of major and minor psychoactive medications—began in 1943 when a Swiss research chemist named Albert Hofman had a dramatic and totally unexpected personal experience with LSD. While at work synthesizing a series of new experimental compounds, he ingested a minute quantity of the drug and, feeling quite strange soon afterward, he went home to lie down. "There surged upon me an uninterrupted stream of fantastic images of extraordinary plasticity and vividness and accompanied by an intense, kaleidoscopelike play of colors," he later wrote. "... I had great difficulty in speaking coherently, my field of vision swayed before me, and objects appeared distorted like images in curved mirrors ... Occasionally, I felt as if I were out of my body ... every sound evoked a corresponding colored hallucination constantly changing in shape and color."

The fact that certain species of mushroom and cactus, coca, and other naturally occurring plants could cause hallucination if eaten or smoked was well known, but the extraordinary response of Dr. Hofman's mind to roughly one three-millionth of an ounce of a chemical compound opened up a new area of scientific investigation. If such an infinitesimal quantity of LSD could cause a schizophreniclike state, did that mean that schizophrenia was chemical? Could insanity be caused by improperly functioning brain cells which produce a chemical reaction much like the reaction Dr. Hofman experienced? Did such suppositions indicate that brain chemistry controls your way of looking at things? Could drugs be developed which would alter and cure the distorted thinking and perceptions of the mentally ill?

Late nineteenth- and early twentieth-century theories that mental illness was due to organic causes formed the basis for profound pessimism about the possibility of cure, because nothing was known about altering inborn defects. Today so much is understood about chemical changes in the cells that research in psychopharmacology offers immense promise. Early experiments with LSD focused the interest of researchers in a number of countries on the search for a biochemical explanation of mood and behavior. The active agent of any drug is chemical, and when taken into the body by mouth or by intravenous injection it works by interacting with the molecules of living matter. The "psychoactive" drugs work in the brain cells and central nervous system to stimulate, depress, or distort their activity. Precisely *how* this occurs is not yet known, but in 1953 an English scientist found that LSD inhibits serotonin in the brain. Serotonin is one of a group of organic compounds known as biogenic amines which are manufactured in the body and function at nerve endings to transmit electrical signals across the gap (synapse) from one nerve cell to another. Soon afterward experiments with the drug reserpine indicated that presence or absence of serotonin in the brain was implicated in studies of mania and depression as well as schizophrenia.

In the mid 1950s Chlorpromazine (Thorazine), a medication designed to reduce anxiety in patients facing surgery, was also found to be involved in the release of serotonin and was soon being used in larger doses to calm deranged patients. Iproniazid, a newly developed drug for tuberculosis, turned despondent patients in sanatariums into euphoric gigglers and singers who literally began to dance in the halls of the hospitals. It was noted that Iproniazid *raised* the serotonin level in the brain. Cocaine, which Freud had acclaimed as a euphoriant, was found to have similar characteristics. Other investigations centered on a new drug for treating Parkinson's disease, L-Dopa, which was also found to be a mood elevator.

Although a great deal remains unknown about the biochemical basis of psychosis, researchers feel that levels of certain biogenic amines are low at particular brain sites in people suffering from depression, high in those who are manic. It is thought that a predisposition toward chemical imbalances may be hereditary. Researchers found, as a missing puzzle piece, that the brain's limbic system—the seat of the emotions—has a high content of several biogenic amines. Favorable results of electroshock therapy on people suffering from depression might be explained by the fact that one result of shock therapy is elevation of the level of the biogenic amine norephinephrine in the brain.

One of the most effective of the psychoactive drugs is lithium, a chemical which seems to be highly successful in treating manic states of manic-depressive psychosis and is also used to halt return of depressions. Older medications which were helpful in treating mania had the undesirable effect of binding the victim in what has been referred to as a "chemical straitjacket"—calming him by placing him in a state of drugged stupefaction. Lithium has been found to control excitability and restlessness without dulling intellectual capability, permitting the patient to function and to be receptive to other forms of therapy.

Lithium, a simple chemical and the third element on the periodic table, was used unsuccessfully against gout, rheumatism, and kidney stones in the mid-nineteenth century. In the 1940s it reappeared as a salt substitute, but was found dangerous for people with kidney and heart disease and was withdrawn. Its psychoactive properties were first discovered in 1949 by John F. J. Cade, an Austrian psychiatrist. Experiments were carried out with confirmatory success in a number of European countries but it was not licensed in the United States until 1970. It is not known as yet how lithium is able to relieve mental illness, but the chemical is believed to operate at the level of information transmission in the brain.

Investigations and discoveries in the biochemical approach to mental illness have involved the efforts of scientists from a wide range of specialties. Historically, it has been only a century and a half since the subject of mental illness became—in the early asylums—the exclusive and indisputable province of psychiatrists. Today, biochemists, neurochemists, psychopharmacologists, geneticists, neurophysiologists, metabolic specialists, and a growing number of researchers from allied fields are cooperating in an interdisciplinary attack on the mysteries of the link between body chemistry and psychosis. Biochemical research into mental illness is still at the fact-finding and fact-gathering stage. Researchers are following up each lead, compiling a vast body of related observations and discoveries that may someday fit together into a comprehensive explanation of why and how mental illness occurs and how it can be totally cured or even prevented.

Interestingly, Freud himself predicted that a biochemical basis for psychosis would someday be found, although the state of scientific investigation of his day offered insufficient techniques to carry out such research. Today medications for mental illness range from the major drugs used to combat psychoses to a host of minor tranquilizers, sedatives, muscle relaxants, and antidepressants. In addition to bringing about the release of patients from mental hospitals, the antipsychotic drugs have radically reduced the use of restraints for those still hospitalized and have been a major factor in the development of the "open hospital" system, in which doors are unlocked and patients stay voluntarily. Because these drugs reduce agitation, cause a decrease or cessation of hallucinations, and leave the patients able to organize their thoughts, they also render them more receptive to other forms of therapy aimed at easing readjustment to life in the community. Today an increasing number of antipsychotic medications are used in varying dosages to treat acute or chronic conditions, and for the maintenance of patients who are in remission from their illness. Many patients find themselves feeling so well that a major problem is that of seeing that they continue to take their pills after they have left the hospital.

In the management of neurotics, there is considerable difference of opinion among psychiatrists about combining drug therapies and psychotherapies. Drugs which decrease restlessness and irritability, promote a feeling of relaxation, and allow the patient to withstand unpleasant emotions are seen by some as a hindrance to psychotherapy. Many believe that the drugs mask symptoms; other therapists find that in relieving anxiety, they allow patients to explore painful emotions and unpleasant memories from which they would ordinarily withdraw.

The uses and abuses of mood-altering drugs by large segments of our population are the subject of constant debate and discussion. The fact that many adults in this country regularly consume tranquilizers, stimulants, and sedatives prescribed by family physicians, gynecologists, surgeons, internists, and other medical specialists is a frequent subject of newspaper and magazine articles. There is unresolved debate about whether this extraordinarily prevalent dependence on "uppers" and "downers" reflects the fact that we live in a stress-producing society or simply that people are increasingly unwilling to attempt to cope with stresses which are an unavoidable aspect of life. Considerable disagreement exists among authoritative medical researchers about the desirability of prescribing drugs for calming hyperactive schoolchildren, for quieting elderly people in nursing homes, and for dulling the appetites of people in weight-reduction programs.

But despite a multitude of unforeseen problems, the original promise of the psychoactive drugs has been fulfilled. In the past two decades vast changes have taken place in the outlook for people afflicted with what have always been the mental illnesses most difficult to treat. Hundreds of thousands of former mental patients who seemed doomed to remain institutionalized for life now live and work in the community as the result of treatment with drugs. The biochemical approach to understanding the workings of the mind has also led to new speculations and findings in the search for a genetic explanation of mental illness. Today the view of most scientists is that personality and mental health are the result of interaction between a person's innate physical qualities and the type of environment in which he matures. The idea that major mental illnesses have both biological and psychological causes is not new, but recent statistics seem to confirm what was previously only theoretical. Studies have demonstrated that there is about a 16 percent risk that the offspring of schizophrenic parents will also develop the disease. In identical twins, who share precisely the same genetic heritage, initial research showed that when one twin became schizophrenic, the other would also in 86 percent of the cases. Newer studies indicate a lower incidence but the hereditary influence is unquestioned today. In fraternal twins, the likelihood that the healthy twin will develop the disease is only 14 percent, the same probability that applies to siblings who are not twins.

Of course, members of a family also share certain environmental influences, as researchers are quick to point out. Pellagra, which causes physical and mental symptoms, was noted to occur in families and was therefore once thought to be hereditary. When it was discovered to result from improper diet, researchers became more alert to the fact that families share genes—*and* a wholesome or unwholesome environment. Later twin studies sought to eliminate this factor. Adopted children, and adults adopted in early life, have been studied to see if statistics on mental illness in brothers and sisters who share genetic, but not environmental, heritages seem to confirm the crucial role of heredity.

"Nature versus nurture" used to be a favorite subject of debate. The contemporary view is that nature *and* nurture combine to make us healthy or to make us ill. There is today total acceptance of the fact that broad attacks on mental illness must be directed at greater understanding of both influences.

Psychosurgery

No organic therapy for mental illness has ever become so dramatically controversial as psychosurgery, also known as "psychiatric neurosurgery." In the popular fictional account, *One Flew Over the Cuckoo's Nest*, by Ken Kesey, Randle Patrick McMurphy, who is unsubdued by psychotherapy, pills, and electroshock, loses in his power struggle with Big Nurse when he is lobotomized. In recent years medical and lay critics have gone to battle against psychosurgical procedures on scientific, legal, and ethical grounds. In 1973 a meeting of the fifth International Congress of Neurological Surgeons in Tokyo was disrupted by protesting Japanese psychologists and students, because the host, a well-known Japanese neurosurgeon, was promoting and performing psychosurgery on disturbed hyperactive children. Prison officials have suggested that the behavior of repeat criminal offenders be altered by experimental neuro-surgical procedures, and the moral questions involved have touched off other heated controversies.

Although drug therapy and electroshock also seek to alter behavior by direct physical assault on the brain, the surgical approach to mental illness has become much more alarming in its implications and potential for misuse. Simply stated, this is because surgery is irreversible. Although some undesirable side effects have been noted in the use of drug and shock treatments, generally they have disappeared when routines are modified or discontinued. Often, striking beneficial results so clearly outweigh disturbing side effects that they become easily acceptable.

Psychosurgery, however, is an extremely radical form of treatment. Brain cells, once destroyed, do not regenerate. Since this is the intent of all psychosurgical procedures—removal of part of the brain or permanent destruction of certain pathways in the brain—it is the most drastic procedure for controlling behavior. Although in theory such surgery is designed to destroy areas of the brain which control undesirable behavior while leaving intellection unimpaired, the results, after decades of increasingly refined surgical technique, are still highly debatable. It was recommended for a wide range of mental illnesses and behavior problems from 1936 to 1955, but it is now used in this country almost exclusively as a last resort.

Historically, surgery for mental illness never advanced beyond the primitive stage of drilling holes in the skull until the 1930s. The idea that surgery might be used to alter personality began with clinical observations made by neurologists almost a century earlier, however. The first case to be carefully studied was that of a twenty-five-year-old victim of severe injury. Phineas Gage was at work on the railroad when, during an explosion, a pipe was driven through his skull and into the frontal lobe of the brain (an area directly behind the forehead). He did not become unconscious. He was taken home in an oxcart and was able to walk up several flights of stairs to his boardinghouse room. He soon recovered his strength, although he had lost a considerable quantity of blood, and survived in good health. It was noted, however, that he exhibited evidence of a changed personality, which surprised old friends. For some years he traveled the country with P. T. Barnum, and crowds came to gape at the man who walked around feeling perfectly well with a length of pipe protruding from his head.

During the last third of the century neurologists noted that patients with brain tumors who showed personality changes also had physical destruction of certain areas of the brain, due to their disease rather than to an accident. Brains of such patients eventually studied at autopsy formed the basis of considerable speculation about the relationship between brain anatomy and personality.

The laboratory experiments which preceded the first lobotomies were made by Dr. John Fulton and associates at Yale University in the early 1930s. Dr. Fulton, a physiologist, performed frontal lobotomies on two chimpanzees named Becky and Lucy. After removal of portions of the frontal lobes, he noted certain profound behavioral changes. Becky, who previously had reacted to frustration with temper tantrums, no longer did so. Lucy also showed slowed emotional responses.

Dr. Egas Moniz of Portugal performed the first frontal lobotomy on a human being—an accomplishment which earned him a Nobel Prize. After operating on twenty psychotic patients, Moniz reported seven total cures and eight cases in which formerly violent personalities showed considerable decrease in tensions and in psychotically disordered reasoning. Soon thereafter, Dr. Walter Freeman and Dr. James Watts popularized lobotomies in this country by performing the operations on a large series of patients at the federal mental institution, St. Elizabeth's Hospital, in Washington, D.C.

While some dramatic results were achieved, particularly in elderly agitated depressed individuals, it soon became apparent that the procedure was often accompanied by a significant worsening in intellection. Many patients became not only calm, but mentally dulled, indifferent to personal cleanliness, irresponsible; some were reduced to semi-vegetative states in which they had to be diapered, fed, and supervised at all times. In their book on the procedure, written in 1950, Freeman and Watts accepted the possibility of dulling of intellect. They put forth the opinion, "It is better for the patient to have a simplified intellect capable of elementary acts, than an intellect where there reigns the disorder of subtle synthesis. Society can accommodate itself to the most humble laborer, but it justifiably distrusts the mad thinker."

Not everyone agreed with this view. There was even debate about whether or not the desired psychological improvement was as certain a result as claimed by enthusiasts in this country and abroad.

Nonetheless, between 1936 and 1955, an estimated seventy thousand prefrontal lobotomies were carried out in the United States and Great Britain. Dr. Freeman himself claimed to have performed over thirty-five hundred such operations. Yet by the mid-1950s, psychosurgery had fallen into disrepute. In part this was due to the indiscriminate patient selection. Critics who accepted questionable results with patients considered hopeless had grave reservations when examining cases in which less radical forms of treatment might have brought about improvement. To a great

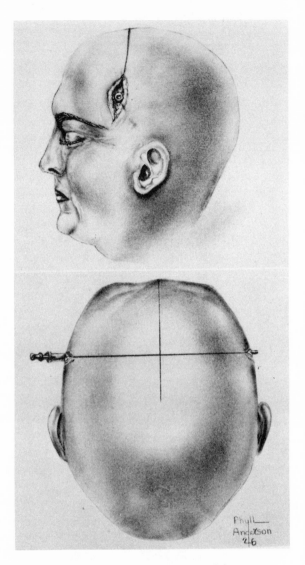

Early lobotomy procedure. From Walter Freeman and James Watts, Psychosurgery, *1950. Courtesy Charles C. Thomas, Publisher.*

extent psychosurgery was rejected, as was electroconvulsive therapy, when the powerful new antipsychotic drugs proved more predictably effective against even the most severe psychiatric problems.

In the 1970s a renaissance has occurred as the result of technological advances. A second generation of psycho-surgeons is experimenting with ever more sophisticated operations which are designed to destroy the least amount of brain tissue in the precisely correct area. The first lobotomies were virtually blind procedures in which large areas of tissue were removed or destroyed by a surgical knife inserted through the orbit (the circle of bone in which the eye is located) or through openings drilled in the skull. Today, brain tissue may be destroyed by freezing probes or by radioactive pellets or, more commonly, through the use of the radio-frequency generator which destroys tissue by heat. Before this takes place electrodes may be implanted in areas of the brain which can then be stimulated to precisely locate centers that produce such behavior patterns as rage states. With the help of precise new brain atlases which provide cross-sectional views, target areas are located, and nerve connections to the limbic system—the part of the brain involved in emotions, which has nothing to do with intellection—can be destroyed. With new instrumentation destruction of tissue can be controlled within a few millimeters.

In actuality, most lobotomies performed today are on totally disabled schizophrenic patients who, often because of violent behavior, present great nursing and management difficulties in hospitals and at home. Usually these are patients on whom all other treatments have failed. With refined technical procedures the likelihood of a lobotomized patient becoming a mental "vegetable" is slight, and most humane people would agree that freeing a man or woman from spending a lifetime raving on a locked ward in a state mental hospital is commendable, even if there is a possibility of some reduction in I.Q. from the operation. Some advocates urge that the range of patients be extended to include hyperactive children, who have been treated by new psychosurgery procedures only to a very limited extent in this country. Psychosurgery has also been recommended for criminals and for addicts. It has even been suggested as recently as 1970 as a "cure" for homosexuality, which many psychiatrists now view as an alternate choice of life-style rather than as an illness.

And yet, many surgical and moral questions persist. Psychiatrists and psychologists have been critical of new psychosurgical methods and have demanded evidence of their effects. Some critics see psychosurgery as the most dangerous form of behavior control and a basic assault on individual freedom. Others point out that the potential for behavior control can be much more easily exerted—and abused—by those practicing psychotherapy and drug treatment. Some would like to see all psychosurgery outlawed.

Moral disputes new to our time center on the right to treatment for both the mentally and physically ill—and what is now seen as the equally valid right to refuse treatment. But the mentally ill are very often unable to fully consider questions such as these. All hospitals require that a patient give consent—acknowledged by his signature on a form—before any surgical procedure. The law requires that this be "informed consent"—that the doctor not only ask the patient to sign his name but that he first give him full information about possible dangers of adverse effects of the procedure and then ask for his permission to proceed. When patients are very ill, very young, or of poor intelligence, obtaining informed consent becomes more complicated. If a patient is also irrational it becomes impossible. With young children and with the mentally ill, someone else must sign as an "authorized representative." Since psychosurgery causes irreversible effects that will last a lifetime, this is a grave responsibility indeed.

II
Other Contemporary Therapies

As our concept of mental illness has expanded, so have our forms of treatment. Most of us have heard the names that fill an overflowing grab bag of widely differing and ever-changing therapies designed to treat those who are mentally ill, discontented, restless, alienated, bored. Even mental health professionals find it difficult to sort out this complex of offerings which range from classical Freudian psychoanalysis to behavior modification to couple therapy to whatever is the most recently devised system in the so-called human potential movement and the latest self-help organization. Some of the new therapies may prove to be passing fads; others have been accepted as valuable advances. Alongside the array of professional therapists who treat mental illness, lay therapists trained in the philosophy and techniques of encounter groups, Transcendental Meditation, est, and other similar systems offer increased awareness, happiness, and emotional freedom to all comers. Freud once explained that the aim of psychiatry was to supplant the misery of neurosis with "everyday unhappiness." Many of today's lay therapies promise to replace everyday unhappiness with transcendent bliss.

What do these treatments have in common? The non-organic therapies work at the psychological level to try in some fashion to right faulty past learning and unhealthy adaptation. This is the aim of all forms of therapy, although they may start from entirely different theoretical bases, use very different techniques, and propose specific goals as diverse as total restructuring of the personality—or overcoming the fear of flying or the compulsion to overeat. All therapies have certain other elements in common. They offer to bring about the desired personality change by one or more of several basic methods: suggestion (you will get well if you follow instructions), manipulation (you have the power to alter your personality or your environment), clarification and interpretation (you will achieve insights and self-understanding), and/or catharsis (you will be purged of unwholesome suppressed emotion through verbal or physical expression and release).

Therapies are administered by psychoanalysts, psychiatrists who do not have psychoanalytic training, clinical psychologists, psychiatric social workers and nurses, and counselors—pastoral counselors, lay therapists trained in a particular technique, faith healers and spiritualists, ordinary men and women who have suffered from the same problem and who offer their own personal insights.

A therapist can be—and has been, from the time of the shamans onward—any helpful person, but it is important to note that the field has always been and still is wide open to charlatans. Licensing laws are particularly lax in the area of counseling and, although it is highly illegal to pose as a psychiatrist or any other type of physician, no regulations prevent the use of titles such as marriage counselor, sex therapist, healer, guidance counselor—or limit fees that may be charged.

PSYCHOANALYSIS, the most prolonged and intensive form of "talk" therapy, is practiced exclusively by men and women who are taught first in medical schools, then as psychiatrists in residency programs, and then as psychoanalysts through special training at psychoanalytic institutes. Qualification requires that they themselves be analyzed. They may practice Freudian psychoanalysis as described in chapter 9, or any one of a number of variations on traditional psychoanalytic theory. The so-called neo-Freudian schools of analysis—Sullivan, Fromm, Adler, Rank, and Horney are the major names associated with this movement—developed as rebellions from what had become accepted Freudian doctrine. Neo-Freudian analysts vary widely in doctrine and approach but most use the couch less than their Freudian colleagues, encourage the analyst to take a more active role, focus less on free association and repressed childhood experiences and more sharply on pinpointing unrealistic attitudes and how they affect everyday situations. Since psychoanalysis is an education, not simply a medical treatment to cure symptoms, it has been most successful with patients who are anxious to be cured and who are intellectually capable of cooperation. Men and women who seek psychoanalytic treatment must have an intact sense of reality and not be too sick to respond to the method, goals, and length and frustrations of treatment. They must also be prepared to commit themselves—emotionally and financially—to treatment involving three to five weekly sessions for a period of two to five years.

The selection of other therapeutic approaches discussed below have all developed since the advent of psychoanalysis, some in the recent past. They can be viewed, in the most general sense, as variations from, developments of, or reactions against Freudian theory and method—the first and still the most influential of the scientific therapies for mental illness. Freudian theory and method, originally greeted as the most shocking and radical set of ideas ever to emerge from a responsible medical mind, has now become—and been attacked as—the conservative establishment approach. It is usually described as *classical* Freudian psychoanalysis.

PSYCHOTHERAPY is an inclusive term indicating therapy based on verbal exchange between patient and therapist. All psychotherapies aim to eliminate psychological and physical symptoms of mental illness through "talking things out." The term, as used today, also indicates that the treatment will focus on understanding specific problems the patient is currently experiencing in everyday life, rather than uncovering and altering the deep underlying bases for neurotic behavior and response as in intensive psychoanalysis. Psychotherapy is practiced by psychiatrists, psychologists, psychiatric social workers and nurses, and other mental health specialists.

In addition to full-scale analysis, most psychoanalysts also practice psychoanalytically oriented psychotherapy, a relatively short-term type of treatment in which the therapist tries to help the patient deal with a current problem or crisis. Even in such brief treatment as one or a few sessions, however, the psychoanalyst will help the patient deal with his problem by understanding his feelings and his defenses and by gaining insight into emotions which cause him anxiety or ambivalence or which he may be denying.

In psychotherapy the therapist will generally sit facing the patient rather than in the traditional psychoanalytic position and will intrude more readily on the patient's self-analysis. He may treat the patient individually or in a group. Unlike psychoanalysis, psychotherapy of one sort or another has been used to treat patients with every form and degree of mental illness.

GROUP PSYCHOTHERAPY is a relatively recent but very fast-growing type of therapy in which patients are treated in the company of others. Group therapy is not simply a setting and technique for treating individuals in a more economical fashion than is possible in individual therapy, although this is a very real consideration. The concept behind group therapy is that one relates not simply to oneself and one's past but to others, and that healing can take place effectively in a group situation. The behavior and attitudes of healthy people are influenced by the responses of their peers, and group psychotherapy applies this to the treatment of the mentally ill. The predominant modern medical view that healing takes place most effectively in the confidential one-to-one relationship of doctor and patient is basic to psychoanalysis but is now being challenged by many therapists. Particularly when patients have strikingly disordered relationships with others, many professionals feel that group therapy is the treatment of choice. This "new" idea underlies healing practices in primitive societies, which are always group affairs involving patient, shaman, and other members of the community.

Some psychiatrists treat members both in individual sessions and in weekly group meetings. Others rely only on group sessions, during which members talk to the therapist and to each other, acting out feelings that might not emerge as readily in individual psychotherapy. The patient observes his own behavior in the group—the way he responds to other members and the way they respond to him. He also observes the interactions of others in the group. The group can consist of people who are very severely or only mildly disturbed, but in all cases patients will be carefully screened before being placed because the group's proper composition is seen as being of the greatest importance.

Many therapists are enthusiastic about group treatment of adolescents, particularly those who are withdrawn from their peers. A common experience in group therapy is that patients who are suffering severely from repressed emotions or from secret acts or thoughts they view as sinful or shameful find, in very short order and to their immense relief, that others in the group are having similar experiences. Group psychotherapy has been tried with patients in every category of mental illness, including the most disturbed schizophrenics. Many patients who have previously made poor progress in individual psychotherapy do well in groups—although the reverse is equally true.

FAMILY THERAPY is a form of psychotherapy which began in this country in the 1960s and has become a specialty of more and more psychiatrists, psychologists, and social workers. Although families usually come to therapy because one of the members is exhibiting symptoms of disturbed personality or unacceptable behavior, family therapists proceed from a concept of troubled families rather than the idea that one family member is disturbed. They approach the family as a unit, a behavior system in which members have established certain ways of reacting to one another's emotional needs and to their own family roles. The immediate problem may center on the behavior of an adolescent member of the family, although in some cases marital discord or the psychotic, neurotic, or addiction problem of one or both of the parents becomes the catalyst. Current crises in the lives of the parents are often reflected in serious behavioral problems in the children, so that pinpointing the "sick" member of the family—which therapists go to great lengths to discourage in all cases—becomes impossible.

Regardless of the specific problem which brought the family to seek help, the therapist attempts to alter patterns of interaction so as to relieve emotional stresses and improve the health of individual family members and the family as a whole. After cutting through accusations and deeply ingrained defenses, the therapist tries to shed illumination on destructive family conflicts and help members find more appropriate methods of coping, encouraging sensitive and concerned approaches which will promote harmony and creative growth.

Technically, family therapy works like other group therapies. The entire nuclear family comes for sessions with the therapist, usually once a week. Interviews with individual members may be combined with these group sessions and other family members—grandparents, uncles, aunts, or even non-family members who play a significant role in the family structure—may be included in the group. Pastoral counselors, educators, and people concerned with counseling adolescents in the police and court system are becoming increasingly aware of the potential benefits of family therapy, and they refer many cases to family therapists.

COUPLE THERAPY treats husband and wife together in an attempt to alter not simply the perceptions and behavior of either member, but also their interaction. Advocates of couple therapy feel that treating one member without including the other does not attack the dynamics of the marriage or illuminate the ways in which intermarital conflicts and habitual types of responses can interfere with genuine emotional closeness. Some therapists involve couples with other troubled couples in small or large groups in which patients speak, as in all forms of group therapy, both to other group members and to the therapists, interacting in a range of combinations and benefiting from the interactions of others. Some therapists are willing to become involved in decisions about whether an unhappy marriage should continue; many others are not.

BEHAVIOR MODIFICATION THERAPY aims directly at changing the way people act, unlike psychotherapy, which is basically concerned with altering thoughts and feelings. Whereas Freudian psychiatrists treat behavior problems as signs of deep-seated emotional conflict, behavior-oriented therapists view virtually all undesirable behavior as habits which, once learned, can be unlearned.

A patient seeking behavior modification treatment must have a clearly defined problem, rather than a complaint such as feelings of alienation, depression, or other diffuse emotional disturbances. The therapist focuses directly on the problem—whether it is sexual dysfunction, phobia, alcoholism, stuttering, nail biting. If the patient complains of alcoholism, he will be considered cured if after treatment he is able to control his drinking. No attempt will be made to unearth the psychological problem which led to his addiction.

Behavior modification is a technique—or, more accurately, a set of techniques—for altering behavior by a system of rewards and punishments. Unacceptable behavior is discouraged (subjected to negative conditioning); good behavior is rewarded (given positive reinforcement). Negative conditioning may take the form of aversion control, which is the imposition of a punishment in the form of a negative stimulus. Brief, low-voltage electric shocks have been used to cure the habit of bed-wetting and to help psychotic patients control the urge to injure themselves. Drugs like Antabuse, which causes violent nausea and vomiting when alcohol is consumed, have been used to teach alcoholics sobriety. The rewards that constitute positive reinforcement vary with the age and inclinations of the person in treatment—money, praise, food, the opportunity to go to a ball game or watch television. Ultimately, it is expected that the newly acquired "correct" behavior will be maintained because it results in a happier life—in other words, is positively reinforced.

Other forms of behavior modification therapy include systematic desensitization, in which patients are gradually exposed under controlled conditions to situations they find threatening in order to combat unreasonable fears and revulsions, and assertiveness training, which involves play-acting in imaginary but commonplace situations which teach people to stick up for their rights.

The applications of this therapy are many and varied. It has been successfully used as a method of dealing with phobias and addictions, compulsive behavior, insomnia, stuttering. Institutionalized retardates and psychotics have been taught to control self-destructive behavior and to take care of personal needs. Hyperactive children have been taught to concentrate on their school assignments. Delinquents have unlearned the habit of assaulting people and stealing. The grossly overweight have been retrained in proper eating habits. People to whom a fear of airplanes means giving up a job involving frequent travel have been cured of their phobia.

Unlike the psychoanalyst, who wants his patient to be as free of his influence as possible, the behaviorist encourages his patient to accept his influence in order to bring about desired changes. Current controversies about behavior modification involve the use of these techniques to control or manipulate people. Critics have pointed out that behavior modification therapy in prisons, which purportedly teaches behavior that will help the prisoners once they are released, often simply teaches submission to authority.

SEX THERAPY is a recent specialty, designed specifically to help people who have problems relating to sexual performance. It is based in behavior modification theory, rather than in psychotherapy. While traditional psychotherapists have dealt with sexual maladjustments by exploring underlying psychological causes, viewing problems in sexual function as symptoms of much deeper neuroses, researchers William Masters and Virginia Johnson originated a method of attacking the problem directly by attempting to alter sexual behavior without lengthy psychotherapy. The field has expanded enormously since the publication in 1966 of the book *Human Sexual Response*.

Therapists trained in Masters and Johnson's methods or in similar techniques treat husband and wife together even if one partner is relatively free of problems. Patients come because they suffer from some persistent form of sexual dysfunction—most commonly premature ejaculation or impotence in the male or lack of orgasmic response in the female. Cause of sexual dysfunction can range from the most basic how-to-do-it misunderstanding through the entire span of psychiatric disorders. Physical causes of these problems are rare and relatively easily diagnosed.

Most sex therapists operate on the Masters and Johnson model in which the couple is treated by a male-female therapy team. The course of treatment is usually brief and concentrated. Therapists attempt to alter unsatisfactory sexual behavior by providing complete information about sexual function and by offering technical suggestions and advice which has proven helpful for others. Limited psychotherapy may also be offered in interviews with both members of the couple and in individual sessions. Practices vary from therapist to therapist, and as in other forms of treatment, the patient's trust in the therapist and confidence in his ability to effectively offer assistance seem to be essential to success.

It should be noted that before the twentieth century what we now see as forms of sexual dysfunction were not considered to be problems. Today's concept that every adult is entitled to a fulfilling sex life has altered our view of the subject and made sex therapy such a rapidly expanding field.

PRIMAL THERAPY is a cathartic form of treatment originated by psychologist Arthur Janov. His book *The Primal Scream* details his psychological concepts, which center on the belief that neurosis is based on actual pain, produced by an accumulation of hurts incurred from earliest infancy onward.

Janov relates his discovery of the therapeutic effect of screaming out this hurt with the case of a patient he calls Danny. Janov urged the patient, who was being treated in a group therapy session, to call out, "Mommy! Daddy!" As the patient began to do so, "he became noticeably upset. Suddenly he was writhing on the floor in agony. His breathing was rapid, spasmodic; 'Mommy! Daddy!', came out of his mouth almost involuntarily in loud screeches.... The writhing gave way to small convulsions, and finally, he released a piercing, deathlike scream that rattled the walls of my office ... All he could say afterward was: 'I made it! I don't know what, but I can feel!' " Primal therapy was born.

Like the more traditional psychotherapies, primal therapy attempts to put the patient in contact with his own feelings. Unlike Freud, Janov believes that specific actions and attitudes of parents toward children—rather than the child's own desires and fears—are the factors that lead to neurosis. He urges patients, through primal therapy, to gather up this pain and let it overwhelm them and then to release it in episodes of screaming.

Patients in primal therapy are told to devote themselves totally to treatment for three weeks, during which individual sessions are conducted daily for a period of two or three hours. The therapist attempts to help the patient explore his most guarded emotions about his parents. "Instead of allowing him to be obsequious or intellectual, we tell him to fall on the floor, screaming, 'Love me, love me!' directly to his parents," writes Janov.

The three weeks of intensive treatment are followed by primal group therapy for about a six-month period. Unlike other group therapies there is no emphasis on the interaction of group members. Patients who have reached their primal crisis in individual therapy attempt to reach additional states of primal awareness—marked by screaming, writhing, groaning, reenacting birth trauma—and apparently usually succeed. Such emotional crises are the goals of primal therapy, and although others have questioned the long-range effectiveness of the intense emotional purge, Janov feels confident that his method is a cure.

MEGAVITAMIN and ORTHOMOLECULAR THERAPY are two names for the same type of organic treatment. It is based on the belief that schizophrenia is caused by an imbalance in body chemistry, and it attempts, through massive doses of vitamins and through dietary control, to alter this condition. Although psychiatrists and researchers acknowledge the existence of a biological defect of some as yet unexplained nature in schizophrenia, the effectiveness of the megavitamin approach is largely supported by testimonials of patients and by the claims of respected Nobel laureate Linus Pauling.

Pauling, who did not originate megavitamin therapy, has supported the theory that some forms of major mental illness may be caused by vitamin deficiencies even in people who eat a well-balanced diet. He believes that schizophrenics may have a different genetic make-up which makes massive doses of these nutriments a requirement for normal mental health. High doses of a number of vitamins—particularly vitamin B_3—are given by orthomolecular psychiatrists. Dosages of vitamins given in this therapy are truly massive, far exceeding dosages given to correct metabolic disturbances for which such therapies are proven effective. Usually the dietary regime is instituted following other forms of organic treatment, most often electroconvulsive therapy and drug therapy. Hormones may also be given. Proponents of this form of therapy have frequently voiced opposition to treatment by psychotherapy, and may also feel that high-vitamin diets can *prevent* most cases of schizophrenia. Because of these claims the treatment has had considerable publicity in magazines and newspapers.

SLEEP THERAPY, which is popular in the Soviet Union and to some degree in western Europe, is based on the belief that keeping the patient in a state of narcosis—drug-induced sleep—for periods of time ranging from two or three to as many as ten days can cure or vastly improve the health of people with certain types of mental illness. In current European sleep therapies brief reductions in drug dosage permit the patient to eat and use the bathroom at regular intervals, but during most of the period specified he remains in bed sleeping. The technique has not been used to any degree in this country.

Sleep therapy, which was introduced in 1922 as a treatment for psychotics as well as for people suffering chronic anxiety states, derives historically from late nineteenth-century rest cures, which kept people in bed and virtually motionless for as long as six weeks. Hypnotic sleep therapies were also developed to keep patients asleep by hypnotic suggestion for periods of days or even weeks. A variety of neurotic disorders were treated by these methods.

In so-called electrosleep treatment, originated in the USSR, the patient is lulled by low milliamperage current—as little as three-fourths of a milliampere—to altered states of consciousness. The patient feels only a slight tingling through the head and then falls asleep with the low current left on for as much as an hour.

NARCOTHERAPY, also rarely used today in this country, was the treatment of choice for psychiatric battlefield casualties in World War II. Also known as the "Pentothal Interview," it employed intravenous injection of drugs—usually sodium pentothal or sodium amatol—to bring about altered states of awareness and lessened inhibitions. The patient was then urged to "relive" traumatic war experiences by recounting them to the therapist. Intended as a short-term therapy for crisis situations, it was based on the belief that if the disturbed soldier could face the painful memories of experiences which brought on his psychological disturbance, he could relieve himself of his crippling anxieties through this catharsis.

HYPNOTHERAPY is a general name for any treatment in which the patient is hypnotized to assist in the search for the roots of neurosis. Hypnotism is often used to help cure people, through suggestion, of addiction to cigarette smoking and other disturbing habits. In the half-waking, half-sleeping hypnotic state subjects are particularly sensitive to the power of suggestion. It is possible to influence a person who is hypnotized to do things or accept attitudes (I do not want to smoke anymore) which ordinarily meet great resistance. Dentists have used hypnotism to produce relaxation and relieve pain, as have obstetricians during childbirth, but most commonly it has been used for psychiatric purposes.

SELF-HELP THERAPIES such as the highly successful Alcoholics Anonymous, Synanon, and Weight Watchers groups work to correct destructive habits such as alcoholism, drug addiction, and overeating with the support of a group of peers. People who have overcome the same problems speak of their struggles and success, offering themselves as models. Meetings of Alcoholics Anonymous begin with a confession as each person in the room says aloud, "My name is ———— (first name only). I am an alcoholic." Through exploring the reasons for their addiction by comparing their life stories with those of others, by the cathartic power of confession, and by the morale boost of group support, great numbers of addicts have been cured in these organizations. Usually no professional leadership is involved, and some groups eliminate leaders altogether. Feminist consciousness-raising groups—although they are not concerned with problems of addiction—offer therapy to people who have suffered from similar handicapping patterns of response by similar methods of confession and release among peers.

ENCOUNTER THERAPY and THE HUMAN POTENTIAL MOVEMENT are names commonly used to cover a constantly expanding list of lay therapies designed to promote happiness, a sense of fulfillment, increased emotional and bodily awareness. Most programs center on a limited but intense exposure to a group experience which may last a weekend, two consecutive weekends, or as long as the Arica Institute's forty-day intensive resident program. Although many people who are currently mentally ill or who have been in more traditional forms of therapy are attracted to attend, these courses of instruction are directed at the general population—all people who seek some inward change, more meaning in life, greater ease in relating to others. Leaders are trained not in psychiatry but in the particular philosophy and technique of the organization—Transcendental Meditation, the Arica Institute, Silva Mind Control, est (Erhard Seminars Training), etc. Emphasis is placed on loss of inhibitions, rapid relief from hang-ups, and increased personal happiness in the present, not in some distant future. Often cleansing and energizing of the body through special exercises and diet are part of an integrated program aimed at physical and emotional awareness and well-being.

The movement began on the west coast with a broad span of alternative courses offered at the Esalen Institute at Big Sur. The early encounter groups, which appear to have reached their peak of popularity in the late 1960s, offered release from repressed feelings through instant intimacy with strangers, through touching, nude swimming, arm wrestling, massage, frank verbal encounters, shouting, cursing, and a general unleashing of restraints. Today these methods for shaking inhibition remain but there is added interest in more structured approaches, in meditation, and in techniques and concepts derived from Eastern religions.

12
The Full Benefits of Our Society

Jean Etienne Dominique Esquirol, the leading French physician of his day, wrote in 1838, "It will often be necessary to vary, combine and modify the means employed; for there is no specific treatment of insanity."

Today most psychiatrists would agree with Esquirol's pronouncement. Although unprecedented advances have been made in the understanding of the effects of environmental stresses on mental health and the physiological and biochemical processes of the brain, there is still no one treatment for either psychotic or neurotic ailments to which all patients respond. Therapies are varied, combined, and modified, and most therapists have very consciously adopted ideas from a number of different sources.

The selection of contemporary therapies presented in the last three chapters is by no means all-inclusive. Biofeedback techniques teach people to monitor many of their bodily processes in an attempt to alter physical and mental problems. Transactional analysis uses the "game" technique to help people improve their interactions with others. Gestalt therapy, Rankian therapy, Reichian therapy, and reality therapy are the names of still more theories with their own modes of treatment. Occupational and recreational therapies include such helpful techniques as psychodrama, in which patients act out painful past situations; music therapy, art therapy, dance therapy; and unstressful useful occupation in sheltered workshops. The fact that new treatments for the mentally ill are constantly being introduced reflects added knowledge, a more open-minded and experimental approach—and a shared conviction that no panacea has been found which would make other therapies unnecessary. It also reflects an expanded definition of mental illness which decrees that those who should receive help include many adults and children who were formerly deemed not sick, but depraved—delinquents, alcoholics, drug addicts, as well as children with certain learning and behavioral problems, adults with persistent disturbances of sexual function, and others whose disabilities are now understood to be psychologically based.

It should be noted that new therapies are usually highly successful as practiced by their enthusiastic originators, but that later practitioners are rarely able to repeat these early successes. Soon the new treatment is accepted, not as a cure-all, but as another tool, an alternate approach for attacking certain specific types of problems. To the despairing mentally ill patient the very fact that someone takes an intense interest in his care and feels he will get better is therapeutic in itself, and virtually *any* form of treatment has been found to bring some level of improvement, including intravenous injections of sterile water.

No discussion of the varying ways in which we now attempt to cure or alleviate mental illness can properly conclude without bringing attention to the difficult subject of the relationship of the mentally ill to the law. Whether or not a person receives treatment at all may be determined

Psychodrama. St. Elizabeth's Hospital, Washington, D.C.

Dance therapy session. American Psychiatric Association Archives.

by the laws of his state. Whether or not his right to refuse treatment is honored may also be determined by legislation. Whether indeed he has or should have such a right is not a matter of agreement among medical and legal experts who have given the subject a good deal of informed consideration. Such questions as whether mental illness occurring after marriage can be used as grounds for divorce by the healthy spouse have been subjects of very heated controversy all through this century. Laws differ from state to state, although most do permit such actions in cases when illness is incurable—which is never easily determined—and has persisted from two to five years. The legal status of the insane in criminal actions has been the category of medical-legal dispute which has posed a genuine life or death issue in cases involving homicide or other capital crimes. All these areas of dispute are complicated by the fact that medical and legal definitions of mental illness have been ambiguous in the past and remain frustratingly so today, despite the attempts of jurists, legislators, and psychiatrists to establish useful guidelines.

Even in earlier societies it was apparent that the insane became the concern of legislators in three basic areas: their personal and property rights, their responsibility in criminal actions, their right to personal freedom. It is only in modern times that the last of these issues has become a highly controversial matter.

Historically, society has been most interested in the relationship of the insane person to his property. From Egyptian, Greek, and Roman civilizations onward legislators have decided such questions as whether a mentally ill person has the right to own land, to sell property, to sign a contract, to make a will, to be held accountable for financial decisions made during a period of irrationality. Generally the answer has been no. Roman laws, Talmudic laws, and other early written legislation stripped the insane of many rights and also of many basic responsibilities. They provided laws for establishing guardianship of the insane by parents, grown children, or court-appointed persons. In England in the late Middle Ages the estates of the insane and the mentally retarded were to be annexed to the Crown. The profits from their land were supposed to be used to maintain them and their families. If they returned to sanity remaining funds were to be restored. Today incompetency proceedings are employed—as they were in Rome and in colonial America—to establish whether the sick individual is unable to take proper care of his own property and person. The rights the incompetent person loses are similar to those denied a minor—writing checks, marrying, voting, making business contracts, and the like.

The rulings relating to criminal actions in which the accused may be insane have their basis in Anglo-American legal tradition. The law assumes that adults are capable of free choice in determining their own behavior. If a person chooses to harm another or commit a burglary he is presumed to be responsible for this act. The concept that the insane do not have free will and may be impelled to act in a violent fashion because of their illness has led to our current criminal laws regarding the mentally disabled.

It is in regard to legislation having to do with the person rather than the property of the insane that those authorized to judge and sentence have the most potent authority. When Cornelius Agrippa, a sixteenth-century lawyer and physician, spoke out in Metz against the condemnation of an aged demented woman for witchcraft, he was questioning the right of an inquisitorial court to mete out death sentences to the insane. When his pupil, Johann Weyer, stated publicly that many imprisoned "criminals" needed medical care rather than confinement in jail, he was expressing a view which is still not shared by everyone in our society. When he insisted that a physician was more qualified than a jurist to decide on questions of mental illness, he was taking a position that would not be widely adopted until the early nineteenth century and which would be questioned in court a few decades later.

Our contemporary laws relating to insanity as a defense in criminal actions derive from legislation of the mid-nineteenth century, but early canon law indicated that children and the insane could not commit crimes because they lacked both malice and freedom of will. Earlier still Talmudic law stated that children, deaf-mutes, and the mentally deranged could not be held civilly or criminally responsible. English laws of the thirteenth century echoed this sentiment, without providing any standard for determining sanity. In 1838 an American psychiatrist, Isaac Ray, wrote a book on the subject stating that insane offenders were "irresistibly impelled to the commission of criminal acts while fully conscious of their nature and consequences." His opinion would be cited in 1954 when the United States Court of Appeals for the District of Columbia adopted the Durham Rule.

The rules by which legal sanity is determined have been framed and reframed during the past 125 years. In 1843 in England a man named Daniel M'Naghten, who suffered paranoid delusions and felt pursued by enemies, murdered the secretary of the prime minister, Sir Robert Peel. The celebrated M'Naghten Rule was established at the trial which acquitted him. It said that a person judged criminally irresponsible by reason of insanity must not have known the difference between right and wrong at the time the criminal act was committed. The "right-wrong" test was adopted in Great Britain and in all American jurisdictions except the state of New Hampshire. Today it is used as the only test of legal insanity in fewer than half the states. From the period of its adoption the rule has been the subject of criticism by both doctors and lawyers. It is considered to be based on an obsolete interpretation of insanity which does not take into account the fact that a sick person can know that an act is illegal and morally wrong and still, because of his disease, commit it.

The irresistible-impulse test is used in conjunction with the M'Naghten Test in a number of jurisdictions. The test states that a person may be compelled to commit an illegal act, although he knows it to be wrong, because of an overpowering impulse which is caused by his mental illness.

The Durham Test, which resulted from the burglary trial of Monte Durham in the United States Court of Appeals for the District of Columbia in 1954, states that the accused is not responsible for his criminal act if the act "was the product of a mental disease or a mental defect." Essentially, this point of view echoes the New Hampshire Supreme Court ruling of 1871, which framed similar legislation when rejecting the M'Naghten ruling as inadequate. It was acclaimed by psychiatrists at first but it was legislatively adopted only in Maine and the Virgin Islands and was specifically rejected in over twenty states and most federal circuits because of difficulty in defining the terms "mental disease" and "product."

The Model Penal Code, drafted by leading legal and mental health authorities, seeks to solve all ambiguities and has been widely adopted. It states that "a person is not responsible for criminal conduct if at the time of such conduct as a result of mental disease or defect he lacks adequate capacity either to appreciate the criminality of his conduct or to conform his conduct to the requirements of law." It then defines the terms "mental disease" and "mental defect."

The point of all these legal tests is to protect both the insane defendant and society. Is the deranged perpetrator of a criminal action less likely to repeat his crime in later years if he is sent to prison or treated in an institution for the criminally insane? It is interesting to note that in the Scandinavian countries no legal definition of insanity is thought necessary and determination of responsibility is made in each case by medical experts. Some legal authorities in this country believe that the much-disputed standards are not necessary here, pointing out that regardless of the wording of the test juries use their own criteria, asking themselves whether the accused acted peculiarly during or after committing the crime. It is important to remember that no one is asked to stand trial if he is not judged competent at the time. If he is too sick to be able to participate in his own defense he will be put in a hospital and the trial will be postponed. The jury is, therefore, faced with a rational man or woman who is said to have been mentally ill at the time of the commission of the crime. Usually expert testimony is introduced on both sides. Although many people fear that hordes of dangerous criminals are spared punishment because of real or presumed mental illness, it is statistically proven that only 5 percent of insanity defenses are upheld.

Laws regarding involuntary hospitalization (commitment) procedures are of relatively recent origin. Previous to the large-scale construction of asylums no one questioned the right of the police or of families or friends—or enemies—to hand over to jailers those they deemed insane and likely to harm others. The unagitated, quiet, withdrawn patients were generally left at liberty. In France Esquirol was the promoter of an advanced 1838 Lunacy Law which established commitment proceedings, requiring signatures of competent physicians followed by a certifying court action. The law inspired similar legislation in other European countries. In England and America the signature of one physician was sufficient to have a person confined to a lunatic asylum. Often this was the signature of the medical superintendent of the asylum, to whom the afflicted person was taken by family or by the police. A husband's allegation that his wife was insane was usually sufficient evidence for confinement.

In the second half of the nineteenth century a number of cases involving false commitment were brought to the courts by former patients, and several were successful. In 1845 one Josiah Oakes alleged illegal commitment. Oakes, an elderly man, was taken to the McLean Asylum in Massachusetts by his children when he became engaged to a young woman of uncertain morals within days of the death of his wife. The judge did not deny that Oakes had exhibited poor judgment in his personal affairs, but ruled that a man could only be deprived of his liberty if by going at large he was a danger to himself and others. In 1849 a man named Hinchman sued his mother, his sister, and the physicians who treated him at the asylum, and he won his case.

The most famous false commitment proceeding was instituted and won by Mrs. Eliza Packard, who had been received and confined in the Illinois State Hospital in 1860. Her book, published after her release from the institution three years later, was titled *Great Disclosures of Spiritual Wickedness in High Places. With an Appeal to the En-*

vironment to Protect the Inalienable Rights of Married Women. It was widely read. As Mrs. Packard told the tale, her husband, a Calvinist minister with whom she had violent religious disagreements, wanted her to sign a deed allowing him to sell some real estate of which she was a partial owner. When she refused he took his wife of twenty-one years—the mother of his six children—to the state asylum in Jacksonville, Illinois, and had her committed. Mrs. Packard brought her case against her husband and the superintendent of the asylum. She went on to crusade for commitment procedures by jury trial.

The immediate result was the passage of the "personal liberty bill" or "Packard Law" in Illinois in 1867, which required that a jury establish insanity before a patient could be confined to an institution. Psychiatrists were quick to point out that requiring the sick person to stand trial was a violation of his privacy and dignity, and that the use of terms like "the accused," "charges," "verdict," lent the proceedings all the stigma of criminal actions. They also felt that juries of lay people were not qualified to pass on mental health or illness, but laws similar to the Illinois law were enacted in states around the country.

Today most states still have involuntary commitment procedures of some sort, either by medical certificate or by jury trial, which is far less common than it used to be. It is the official opinion of the American Civil Liberties Union that the standards for involuntary commitment are unconstitutionally vague and that no one should be deprived of personal liberty under such rulings. Many psychiatrists, however, feel that new commitment procedures are unnecessarily stringent, making it impossible to hospitalize people too sick to act voluntarily in their own best interests and those of their families. There is increased emphasis on voluntary admission to "open" hospitals, where doors are not locked and patients are not restrained from leaving. The open hospital system began in England and Scotland in the 1940s and was initiated in this country a decade later. There are also today approximately five hundred psychiatric units in general hospitals where psychiatric patients are free, as are other patients in the hospital, to sign out—even if they do so against medical advice. The authoritative Group for the Advancement of Psychiatry estimates that 10 percent of the mentally ill may still require treatment on an involuntary basis, whereas 90 percent of those requiring hospitalization could be admitted voluntarily or on a temporary emergency basis.

On June 26, 1976, a unanimous United States Supreme Court decision decreed that it is no longer permissible to confine in custodial institutions mentally ill but harmless individuals who are "capable of surviving safely in freedom," either alone or with friends or family. Kenneth Donaldson, a sixty-seven-year-old man who had spent fifteen years in a state mental hospital in Florida, brought suit and was freed after his case reached the Supreme Court. It was the first time in this century that the Supreme Court of the United States had ruled on the constitutional rights of mental patients committed in civil procedures. Donaldson, who for many years had been suffering from delusions that people were poisoning him, spreading evil rumors about him, and stealing his ideas, was brought to the state hospital by his parents, where he was diagnosed as a paranoid schizophrenic. For years he wrote to senators, congressmen, lawyers, and doctors, attempting to secure his release. After endless frustrations he found a physician-attorney interested in the rights of mental patients. It is estimated that a quarter of a million people who, like

Donaldson, are not dangerous and are not receiving treatment, are being held in mental institutions at this time.

The unanimous decision in the Donaldson case reflects
a changing view of personal liberty which now includes
those citizens who have always been routinely deprived of
civil rights—the mentally ill. It also reflects the fact that
today there are alternatives to hospitalization including
halfway houses, day hospitals, night hospitals, outpatient
clinics, sheltered workshops. Even seriously ill men and
women are often able to function outside institutions if
they are given a place to live where meals are provided,
medication supervised, some rehabilitative help offered.

When the United States Congress enacted the Community Mental Health Centers Act in October of 1963,
community psychiatry was greeted as "the third psychiatric
revolution"—following the innovations of Pinel and Freud.
Although as far back as 1913 Adolf Meyer had envisioned
community mental health centers which would undertake
preventive, therapeutic, and rehabilitative services, the subject was rarely discussed again until the mid-1950s. Today
the National Institute of Mental Health, established in
1949, conducts research in mental health, supports training
programs for mental health specialists, and assists the states
in developing community facilities to serve the mentally
ill. In the late 1950s NIMH officials selected representatives
from many organizations and disciplines to analyze the
needs of the mentally ill in America and the available
resources.

In 1963 President Kennedy sent to Congress the first
message ever put forth by an American president representing the interests of the mentally ill. In authorizing grants
for the construction of a network of interlocking comprehensive community mental health centers he described

mental illness and mental retardation as critical health problems which "occur more frequently, affect more people, require more prolonged treatment, cause more suffering by the families of the afflicted, waste more of our human resources, and constitute more financial drain both upon the Public Treasury and the personal finances of the individual families than any other single condition." He cited the shameful statistics on care in the custodial state institutions where four dollars is the average amount spent per patient per day, with less than two dollars allotted in

A scene from One Flew Over the Cuckoo's Nest, *one of the many plays with themes concerning mental illness produced in recent years at the Arena Stage, Washington, D.C.*

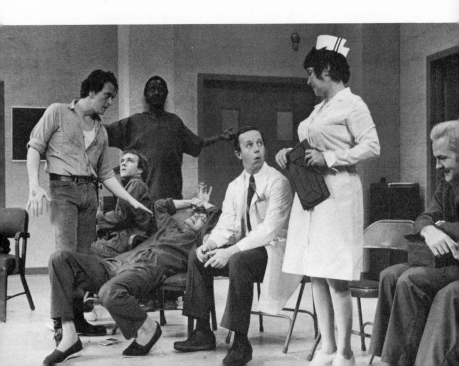

some states. He revealed that in many institutions there is one psychiatrist for every 360 patients. He urged that we, as a nation, cease our neglect and act to "bestow the full benefits of our society on those who suffer from mental disabilities."

Today, due to emphasis on community care and the effectiveness of tranquilizing and antidepressant medication, four hundred thousand mental patients are released each year from state and county hospitals. Because of inadequate funding and neighborhood opposition, community services have not developed as rapidly as envisioned. NIMH listed only 209 halfway houses here in 1976. Heavily populated New York State had only 11. Many former mental hospital patients have been placed by welfare departments in inadequate boardinghouses and foster care facilities. Overemphasis on releasing patients from hospitals has also tended to obscure the fact that for many people who need to escape the pressures of home and community in order to get well, the hospital setting remains a genuine "asylum" and the most therapeutic environment.

Community mental health is still a new concept, but it is bringing vast numbers of our mentally ill citizens from isolated institutions back into the cities and towns. People who were once hidden from view now pass us on the street and sit with us on the bus. Perhaps one day the full benefits of our society *will* be extended to its most vulnerable citizens, the mentally ill. Meanwhile the very fact that community placement has made these "different" people more visible should inevitably lead to greater public understanding and compassion for their problems—and enrich the humanity of us all.

Suggestions for Further Reading

The following books all relate to the broad subject of mental illness. Some are fiction, some nonfiction, and many are based on the firsthand experiences of mental patients.

Beers, Clifford W. *A Mind That Found Itself: An Autobiography*. Rev. ed. New York: Doubleday & Co., 1948.
> Originally published in 1908, this autobiographical account of Beers's struggle to recover from mental illness in both public and private institutions was the first of its kind. Beers became the leader of the mental health movement, and his book and his work inspired widespread new programs and reforms.

Benziger, Barbara F. *Prison of My Mind*. New York: Walker & Co., 1969.
> Moving autobiographical account of a woman's mental breakdown and her fight to regain her sanity.

Berne, Eric. *A Layman's Guide to Psychiatry and Psychoanalysis*. New York: Simon & Schuster, 1975.

Bettelheim, Bruno. *Love Is Not Enough*. New York: Free Press, 1950.
> A book about the treatment of severely disturbed children in the experimental Sonia Shankman Orthogenic School at the University of Chicago.

Burgess, Anthony. *A Clockwork Orange*. New York: W. W. Norton & Co., 1963.
> A novel treating the subject of behavior modification. In

this fantasy of the future negative conditioning is used in an attempt to cure outbreaks of violence.

Cammer, Leonard. *Up from Depression.* New York: Simon & Schuster, 1969.
A psychiatrist discusses the symptoms of depression and current treatments.

Deutsch, Albert. *The Mentally Ill in America.* New York: Columbia University Press, 1949.
This authoritative study was first published in 1937. Thoroughly researched and considered a landmark book in the history of psychiatry.

Ennis, Bruce and Siegel, Loren. *The Rights of Mental Patients.* New York: Avon Books, 1973.

Green, Hannah. *I Never Promised You a Rose Garden.* New York: Holt, Rinehart & Winston, 1964.
A teenaged schizophrenic's three years in a mental hospital. This fictionalized account is based on the author's experiences.

Guest, Judith. *Ordinary People.* New York: Viking Press, 1976.
Following a suicide attempt, a seventeen-year-old boy spends eight months in a mental institution. When he returns home, he and his family learn to come to terms with reality.

Hoffer, Abram, and Osmond, Humphry. *How to Live with Schizophrenia.* Rev. ed. Secaucus, N. J.: University Books, 1974.
This book explains the orthomolecular or megavitamin approach to therapy, one of the most controversial areas in treatment today.

Huxley, Aldous. *Devils of Loudon.* New York: Harper & Row, Publishers, 1971.
In the seventeenth century, young nuns at the convent of Loudon brought charges of bewitchment against the curé Urbain Grandier. Huxley describes the incident and the events that followed.

Jones, Ernest. *The Life and Work of Sigmund Freud.* 3 vols. New York: Basic Books, 1957.
Although there are many "popular" biographies of Sigmund

Freud, this three-volume work remains the classic study. A highly readable account of the man and his enduring contributions.

Kesey, Ken. *One Flew Over the Cuckoo's Nest.* New York: Viking Press, 1962.
A fine novel about the struggle for power in a mental institution.

Pines, Maya. *The Brain Changers: Scientists and the New Mind.* New York: Harcourt Brace Jovanovich, 1973.
Illuminating discussion of scientific research and the issue of mind control.

Plath, Sylvia. *The Bell Jar.* New York: Harper & Row, Publishers, 1971.
A fictionalized account of the mental breakdown of the highly gifted poet.

Rubin, Theodore I. *Jordi; Lisa and David.* New York: Ballantine Books, 1975.
Two stories, one about a psychotic child, and the other about two mentally ill teenagers who learn how much they have to give to each other.

Stevenson, Robert Louis. *Strange Case of Dr. Jekyll and Mr. Hyde and Other Famous Tales.* New York: Dodd, Mead & Co., 1961.
The classic tale of Jekyll and Hyde (1886) is an early fictional treatment of the subject of split personality.

Vonnegut, Mark. *The Eden Express: A Personal Account of Schizophrenia.* New York: Praeger Publishers, 1975.
Dramatic autobiographical account of a schizophrenic breakdown which occurred while the author, a recent college graduate, was living on a farm in British Columbia. Vonnegut is a proponent of the orthomolecular regime of treatment.

Ward, Mary Jane. *The Snake Pit.* New York: New American Library, Signet, 1973.
This story about the patients in a mental hospital, written in 1946, led to the use of the term "snake pit" to describe the horrors of our worst mental institutions.

Index

Adams, John Quincy, 107
Adler, Alfred, 129, 130, 156
Agrippa, Cornelius, 63, 175
Ajax, 26
Almshouses, 71
Anatomy, 38
Animal magnetism, 107–111
Anxiety, 120
Aristotle, 34–35
Arnauld of Villanova, 58
Asclepiades, 35
Asklepios (god), 30
Astrology, 53–54, 58
Asylums, 9–10, 72–73, 78–99
Aurelianus, Caelius, 36
Autism, 116
Avicenna, 43–44
Awl, William, 90, 105

Bartholomew, 54
Beasts, transformation into, 22–23
Beers, Clifford, 99
Beggars, 79
Behavioral modification therapy, 161–163
Bernheim, Hippolyte, 122
Bini, L., 136
Biofeedback, 171
Bleeding, 29, 36, 68, 72, 74, 100
Bly, Nellie, 98–99
Boleyn, Anne, 59

Brattle, Thomas, 69
Breuer, Josef, 122–124
Brigham, Amariah, 91
Brill, Abraham, 129
Burton, Robert, 66–67

Cade, John F., 143
Celsus, Cornelius, 36
Cerletti, Ugo, 136
Charcot, Jean Martin, 114, 121–122
Charles VI, King of France, 53
Chauliac, Guy de, 58
Chlorpromazine (Thorazine), 142
Christian Science movement, 112
Christianity, 39–40, 44–53
Cocaine, 140, 142
Commitment, 178–182
Community mental health, 182–184
Conversion reaction, 120
Couple therapy, 160–161
Cruikshank, George, 10

Dance manias, 48, 49
Darwin, Erasmus, 74
David, 20, 21
Degeneration, theory of, 96
Dementia, 86
Democritus, 35

Demoniac possession, 17–19, 51–53

Depression, 119–120, 134, 138

Depressive psychosis, 116, 117

Deutsch, Helen, 129–130

Dickens, Charles, 89

Dix, Dorothea Lynde, 93–95

Donaldson, Kenneth, 181–182

Dreams, 18, 127

Drugs, 11, 38, 113, 133, 134, 140–147

Durham Test, 177

Dymphna, Saint, 47

Eagleton, Thomas, 138

Earle, Pliny, 105

Eddy, Asa Gilbert, 112

Electroconvulsive (electroshock) therapy (ECT), 11, 133–140

Encounter therapy, 154, 169–170

Endomorphs, 133

Epilepsy, 16–17

Esquirol, Jean Etienne Dominique, 171, 179

Est, 154,

Exorcism, 11, 40, 51–53

Faith healing, 16–17, 47–48

Family therapy, 159–160

Ferenczi, Sandor, 129

Flagellation, 48–49

Franklin, Benjamin, 71–72, 134

Frederick II, King of Germany, 57–58

Free association, 125

Freeman, Walter, 150

Freud, Anna, 129

Freud, Sigmund, 33, 114, 117, 121–130, 140, 142, 144

Fromm, Erich, 156

Fulton, John, 149

Gage, Phineas, 148–149

Galen, 37–38, 134

Gall, Franz Joseph, 104, 105

Garfield, James, 105

George III, King of England, 87–88

Gestalt therapy, 171

Graham, James, 102, 111

Grandier, Urbain, 63–64

Gray, John, 96, 97

Greatrakes, Valentine, 48

Greece (ancient), 25–35, 131–132

Group psychotherapy, 158–159

Guiteau, Charles, 97

Halfway houses, 182, 184

Hancock, Thomas, 71

Hashish, 140

Hellebore, 29, 113

Henry VIII, King of England, 59

Heresy, 56–57

Hippocrates, 25, 30–33, 67

Hofman, Albert, 141

Holy relics, 40, 46

Hone, William, 10

Horney, Karen, 129, 156

Human potential movement, 169–170

Hydropathy, 112–113

Hypnotism, 107, 121–123, 125, 168

Hysteria, 32, 33, 37, 114, 115, 120, 122–124

Idiotism, 86

Imhotep, 19

Inquisition, 56–57

Insulin coma treatment, 139

Iproniazid, 142

Irish immigrants, 95–96

James, William, 99
Janov, Arthur, 164–165
Jarvis, Edward, 95
Jauregg, Wagner von, 132
Jeanne des Anges, 63
Jesus, 23–24
Joan of Arc, 56
Johnson, Virginia, 163
Jones, Ernest, 129
Jung, Carl Gustav, 129, 130

Kennedy, John F., 182–184
Kinsey, Alfred, 101
Kirkbridge, Thomas S., 91
Klein, Melanie, 129
Kraepelin, Emil, 132
Kretschmer, Ernst, 133

L-Dopa, 142
Langman, William, 54
Law, 172–182
"Layla and Majnun," 41–42
Lepois, Charles, 66
Leprosy, 14
Lithium, 143
Lobotomies, 147, 149–152
Louis XIV, King of France, 81
Louis XVI, King of France, 108
Lovett, Richard, 134
LSD, 141–142
Lunatic asylums, 9–10, 72–73,
    78–99
Lycanthropy, 22

Malleus Maleficarum, 60–61
Mania, 28–29, 86
Manic-depressive psychosis, 116,
    117, 143
Mann, Horace, 89, 105
Masters, William, 163
Masturbation, 101–102
Medicine men, 16–18

*Medico-Philosophical Treatise
    on Insanity* (Pinel), 85
Megavitamin therapy, 165–166
Melancholia, 28–29, 86
Mesmer, Anton, 107–110, 121
Mesmerism, 107–111
Mesomorphs, 133
Metrazol treatment, 136
Meyer, Adolph, 182
Middle Ages, 39–55
M'Naghten Rule, 176–177
Model Penal Code, 177–178
Moniz, Egas, 149
Montaigne, Michel Eyquem de,
    64
Moslems, 40–44

Narcotherapy, 167–168
National Institute of Mental
    Health, 182
Nebuchadnezzar, King, 21–22
Neo-Freudian analysts, 156
Neurology, 121–122
Neuroses, 116–120, 124, 125,
    128, 129
New Testament, 23–24
Norris, William, 9–10, 12

Obsessive-compulsive neurosis,
    118–119
Occupational therapy, 11, 172
Oedipus complex, 128
Old Testament, 19–23
Opium, 140
Order of the Hospitalers, 81
Orestes, 26
Orthomolecular therapy, 165–
    166

Packard, Eliza, 179–180
Paracelsus, 62–63
Paresis, 132
Pauling, Linus, 166

Pellagra, 133, 146–147
Perkins, Elisha, 111
Personality disorders, 120–121
Phobias, 118, 119
Phrenitis, 33
Phrenology, 104–107
Pinel, Philippe, 83–86
PKU (phenylketonuria), 133
Plagues, 14
Plater, Felix, 66
Plato, 34
Pneuma, 33
Poe, Edgar Allan, 105, 111
Postpartum psychosis, 32
Primal therapy, 164–165
Prophets (Old Testament), 19–20
Psychoanalysis, 33, 115–130, 156
Psychoneurotic phobia, 32
Psychopharmacology (drug treatment), 133, 134, 140–147
Psychoses, 28, 115, 116, 117, 128
Psychosurgery, 11, 133, 134, 147–153
Psychotherapy, 11, 43, 157–158
Puységur, Marquis de, 111

Quakers, 71
Quimby, Phineas Parkhurst, 111–112

Rank, Otto, 129, 156
Rankian therapy, 171
Ray, Isaac, 176
Reality therapy, 171
Recreation therapy, 11, 172
Reichian therapy, 171
Relics, 40, 46
Reserpine, 142
Rhazes, 43
Rome (ancient), 35–38
Rush, Benjamin, 73–74, 76–77, 113

Sachs, Hanns, 129
Sacrifices, 17, 30
Sakel, Manfred, 139
Saul, King, 20, 21
Schizophrenia, 116, 134, 138, 139, 146, 166
Scot, Reginald, 64
Self-help therapies, 168–169
Serotonin, 142
Sex therapy, 163–164
Shamans, 16–18
Sheldon, W. H., 133
Shrines, 30, 46–47
Sleep therapy, 166–167
Soranus, 36–37
Sorcery, 56–64, 68–69
Spurzheim, John Caspar, 104
Stoics, 38
Stone surgery, 53
Straitjackets, 113
Sullivan, Harry S., 156
Syphilis, 14, 132

Talmud, 23
Tranquilizing chair, 74, 76
Transactional analysis, 171
Transcendental Meditation, 154
Transference, 124, 127–128
Trephination, 11, 18, 53, 58
Tuke, Samuel, 87
Tuke, William, 86–87

Ulysses, 26–27

Vesalius, Andreas, 66

Ward, Mary Jane, 99
Watts, James, 150
Weyer, Johann, 63, 175–176
Whitman, Walt, 105
Witchcraft, 56–64, 68–69
Woodward, Samuel, 93

About the Author

ELINOR LANDER HORWITZ has been a freelance writer since her graduation from Smith College. She has been a frequent contributor to the *Washington Post* and the *Washington Star*, has written for many national magazines, and is the author of nine other books for young readers, including THE BIRD, THE BANNER, AND UNCLE SAM. She and her husband, neurosurgeon Norman Horwitz, live in Chevy Chase, Maryland. They have three children.